Molière

L'Ecole des femmes

Noël Peacock

Senior Lecturer in French,
University of Glasgow

University of Glasgow French and German Publications
1989

University of Glasgow French and German Publications

Series Editors: Mark G. Ward (German)
                  Geoff Woollen (French)

Consultant Editors : Colin Smethurst
                     Kenneth Varty

Modern Languages Building, University of Glasgow,
Glasgow G12 8QL, Scotland.

First published 1988; revised and augmented edition, 1989.

© Copyright University of Glasgow French and German Publications
All rights reserved. No part of this publication may be reproduced, stored in a retrieval system, or transmitted, in any form or by any means, electronical, mechanical, recording or otherwise, without the prior permission of the publisher.

Printed by BPCC Wheatons Ltd., Exeter.

ISBN   0 85261 245 1

Contents

Preface		iv
Chapter One	A Controversial Triumph	1
Chapter Two	Structure	4
Chapter Three	The *Ecole* Theme	23
Chapter Four	Comic Language	32
Chapter Five	Commentaries	46
	Act I, Scene 1	46
	Act V, Scene 4, ll. 1586-1611	54
Chapter Six	New Comedy	62
Bibliography		71

Preface

All references to *L'Ecole des femmes* and to *La Critique de L'Ecole des femmes* have been taken from the excellent edition by W. D. Howarth (Oxford, Blackwell, 1963). References to other works contained in the Bibliography have been expressed by the name of the author and the page number where appropriate, except where more than one work appears under the same name, in which case the work referred to is designated by an italicized number corresponding to its position in the Bibliography—e.g. McBride, *26* , p. 12 = R. McBride, *The Sceptical Vision of Molière . A Study in Paradox* , London, Macmillan, 1977, p. 12. Line numbers are supplied in parentheses—IV, 3 = Act IV, scene 3.

My debt to *moliéristes* is impossible to express in a short volume. I should, however, like to record my gratitude to Professor H.T. Barnwell for reading my manuscript and for his invaluable suggestions and encouragement. I am also grateful to the Modern Humanities Research Association for permission to use, in Chapter Four, a modified form of a substantial part of my article, 'Verbal Costume in *L'Ecole des Femmes* ', published in *The Modern Language Review* .

Chapter One

A Controversial Triumph

L'Ecole des femmes has generally been regarded as Molière's first *grande comédie*. Its box-office success was unprecedented: the play had a continuous run from December 26, 1662 to March 9, 1663, and from June 1 to August 12, 1663. It won the approval of the King, and was published in 1663 with a dedication to Madame, Henriette d'Angleterre, the wife of Monsieur, the King's brother.

By 1662, Molière's career as a dramatist had begun to take off. Behind him were the financial problems which had brought an abrupt halt to his first theatrical enterprise, the *Illustre Théâtre*, culminating in his imprisonment for debt in 1645. Behind him, too, the arduous itineraries in the provinces, where he had spent thirteen years after his release from the Châtelet prison. By 1661, Molière had his own theatre, the Palais-Royal, and enjoyed a measure of financial security from the patronage of the King's brother and from the success of his early works. *Les Précieuses ridicules* had taken Paris by storm in 1659. Molière's only failure, *Dom Garcie de Navarre* (1661), had been cancelled out by the success of the two plays which followed it in the same year: *L'Ecole des maris* and *Les Fâcheux*. But it was with *L'Ecole des femmes* that Molière's reputation as a great comic dramatist was to be established.

The critical reception of *L'Ecole des femmes* has, however, been somewhat paradoxical. Though widely acknowledged as a masterpiece, the play did not, until recently, figure prominently on school syllabuses in France. In fact, the 1968 Bordas edition refers to the play as 'une pièce ignorée dans nos classes'. This omission is somewhat ironic in view of the play's central focus on the teaching of ignorance and the fact that its female protagonist, Agnès, is seventeen, the same age as many of its sixth-form readers (see Barbara Johnson, p. 171). The play has also not received the critical attention appropriate to its status in the Molière canon. Each year, the critical bibliography on *Les Précieuses ridicules*, *Tartuffe*, *Dom Juan*, *Le Misanthrope* or *Le Bourgeois gentilhomme* is much more extensive.

In Molière's day, attitudes to the play were polarized. The considerable box-office success was accompanied by a bitter controversy which lasted nearly two years, and which was almost as famous as the one provoked by Corneille's *Le Cid* in 1637. The controversy, which became known as 'La Guerre comique', drew in literary opponents like Donneau de Visé, Boursault and Robinet, rival actors like Montfleury, and moralists and prudes who formed a pressure group referred to subsequently as 'la cabale des dévots'. Some of Molière's antagonists, de Visé, Boursault and Robinet, were later to become his supporters; others, like the *dévots*, stepped up their opposition and were successful in having one of Molière's greatest plays, *Tartuffe*, banned from the stage for five years until 1669.

The "Comic War" provoked by *L'Ecole des femmes* centred on aesthetic, moral and personal issues: the violation of the rules concerning the unities of time and place; inconsistencies within the main character; an "inconsequential dénouement"; plagiarism; licentiousness and obscenity; parody of religion; the attribution of anti-feminism to Molière; and an insinuation that he had married his own daughter.

Molière's *riposte* to his critics took the form not of a scurrilous pamphlet but, appropriately, of a light-hearted dramatic spectacle entitled *La Critique de L'Ecole des femmes*. In it, the charges of his adversaries are mocked by being spoken by three ridiculous characters: the foppish and simple-minded Marquis, whose complaints are trivialized by his self-preoccupation and by his confession to not having listened to Molière's play; the prude, Climène, who preaches (with all the exaggeration one would associate with Molière's comic victims) against what she considers to be the play's immorality and profanity; the author, Lysidas, whose strictures on Molière's literary unorthodoxy are shown to be motivated by pique and jealousy. The defence of Molière's play is entrusted to the "commonsensical" Dorante and Uranie, and to the ironist, Elise, who acts as a kind of *agent provocateur*, inducing Molière's opponents to expose the folly of their polemic.

Molière's *riposte* led to counter-attacks, particularly to Boursault's *Le Portrait du Peintre*. Once again Molière's defence took the form of a theatrical caricature of his adversaries, this time of the actors of a rival company, L'Hôtel de Bourgogne. The counter counter-attack, entitled *L'Impromptu de Versailles*, spawned further *ripostes*. The war was finally concluded on March 17th, 1664 with Philippe de la Croix's defence of Molière entitled *La Guerre comique ou la Défense de l'Ecole des femmes*.

Nowadays, the *querelle* is mainly of historical interest. Nevertheless, the play still divides critics. The central issue has become the question of genre : is the play comic or tragic? or a fusion of comedy and tragedy? Productions at the Comédie-Française have emphasized serious aspects. J. Meyer, in 1959, turned Arnolphe into a 'dyspepsique'; J.- P. Roussillon, in 1973, evolved a curious analogy between Arnolphe and Hitler:

> D'Arnolphe, je fais un monstre, parce qu'il y a trop de gens qui au fond, trouveraient son histoire pas si mal. Je veux qu'il lève le cœur. J'exagère, je n'ai pas tout à fait le sens des mots, mais pour moi c'est Hitler. (see 7, p. 190)

Roussillon's interpreters, P. Dux and M. Aumont, portrayed Arnolphe respectively as 'un anxieux' and as 'un monstre froid'. Others have seen Arnolphe caught up (before his time) in the existentialist's sado-masochistic dialectic. Molière's hero has also been compared with Racine's tragic heroine, Phèdre, with Corneille's hapless victims, Sabine and Camille, and with Kafka's angst-ridden protagonist, Joseph K.

The aim of this study is to review the play as a comedy, bearing in mind Molière's advice to his contemporaries in his preface to *L'Amour médecin* : 'les Comédies ne sont faites que pour être jouées'. I shall consider the play as a script to be performed by actors and before an audience. My primary interest will be to examine how the play works on the spectators—by means of its structure, its language, and its central theme. I shall pay particular attention to questions raised by critics and students, especially those concerning genre, construction, and the function of social and moral aspects. Almost half of the volume will be devoted to Molière's language, which previous studies have tended to neglect or to treat in general terms.

Chapter Two

Structure

(A) STATIC OR DYNAMIC ?

One of the commonest criticisms of the structure of the play from its first performance to the present day has been that it lacks action. One quarter of the play is taken up with *récits* and soliloquies (there are, in fact, fourteen soliloquies and seven *récits*). Furthermore, of the fourteen soliloquies, seven constitute a scene in themselves, and four contain over thirty lines (III, 3 [36 lines]; IV, 7 [34 lines]; III, 5 and IV, 1 [31 lines]). In addition, some of Arnolphe's speeches have been considered too long: his speech in III, 2 extends over seventy-two lines, and is followed by the reading of the *maximes* by Agnès. In fact, according to the 1682 edition, some of Arnolphe's longer speeches were cut in performance (e.g. 649-55, 687-94, 812-19, 822-23, 982-93, 1186-1205).

Molière sought to refute some of these charges in *La Critique* (sc. 6). The argument that the *récits* are tiresome is assigned to the ridiculous poet, Lysidas: 'dans cette comédie-ci (*L'Ecole des femmes*), il ne se passe point d'actions, et tout consiste en des récits que vient faire ou Agnès ou Horace', and countered by the sympathetically portrayed Dorante and Uranie:

> ... les récits eux-mêmes y sont des actions suivant la constitution du sujet; d'autant qu'ils sont tous faits innocemment, ces récits, à la personne intéressée, qui par là entre, à tous coups, dans une confusion à réjouir les spectateurs. [...]
>
> Pour moi, je trouve que la beauté du sujet de *l'Ecole des femmes* consiste dans cette confidence perpétuelle; et ce qui me paraît assez plaisant, c'est qu'un homme qui a de l'esprit, et qui est averti de tout par une innocente qui est sa maîtresse, et par un étourdi qui est son rival, ne puisse avec cela éviter ce qui lui arrive.

Molière derives a comic paradox from his opponents' dismissal of the plot of *L'Ecole des femmes* as slow-moving; his *riposte* is, itself, devoid of any external action and consists of a series of discussions. Hence this defence did not satisfy his contemporaries any more than it has modern critics who have sought to impute to *L'Ecole des femmes* the static nature of plays by Beckett, Pinter or Bennett.

There is a further problem for English-speaking audiences, versed in the action-packed theatre of Shakespeare. Some of the most physically expressive moments of *L'Ecole des femmes* occur off-stage. Horace's first visit to Agnès, the intervention of the *entremetteuse*, the throwing of the stone, the lover's eavesdropping (from a cupboard) on his rival's passionate outburst, Horace's climbing of the ladder and fall, and Agnès's escape might have been represented on stage in Shakespeare. Molière conveys these incidents through a series of narrations by Agnès and Horace.

The overall effect, however, is not one of inertia or of stagnation. Tension and suspense are created for the characters, if not always for the audience, for reasons which will be given in the next section. The impact of the *récits* on the addressee may be considered as more dramatic than if Arnolphe had been subjected to physical torture on stage (see Nina Eckstein, p. 229). Arnolphe's reactions to Horace's news give to the *récits* a theatricality which is often lost in a mere reading of the text. As Hall has suggested (p. 130): 'On Molière's stage the narrative parts of the play were almost more important for what they allow Arnolphe as listener to mime than they are for the verbal content which so dominates the printed page'.

In addition, Molière works variations within the pattern of *récits*. Horace and Agnès recount the same incident from a different perspective (I, 4 and II, 5): Horace focuses on Agnès's unadorned charm and on the folly of her oppressor, while Agnès gives an almost verbatim account of each stage of the visit, thus delaying the disclosure of what Arnolphe most wants to find out. Through Arnolphe's reactions to the two accounts, Molière dramatizes the fluctuating nature of Arnolphe's emotions: from euphoria to despair (I, 4), and from anxiety to relief (II, 5). These widely differing reactions are revealed by Molière's modification of the structure of the *récits*. Sometimes the *récit* is punctuated by numerous interruptions, which make it similar to a dramatic dialogue (see Eckstein, p. 229). For example, in III, 4, Arnolphe interrupts Horace's narrative seven times; four times his questions elicit further information and give added momentum to the *récit* . On other occasions, Arnolphe is more subdued; in IV, 6, even silent.

The dramatic function of Arnolphe's soliloquies is not dissimilar to that of Horace's *récits* . Some are used to refer to Arnolphe's revised strategy (I, 4; III, 5; IV, 5 and IV, 7); others relaunch the plot after the interval between acts (II, 1 and IV, 1). Arnolphe's soliloquies also allow us to penetrate his innermost thoughts and feelings. The secrecy of Arnolphe's plan forces him to dissimulate to everyone except to his friend, Chrysalde. The predominant structure of Arnolphe's soliloquies parallels that of Horace's *récits* : the transition in Arnolphe from despair to optimism reflects the emotional states through which Horace passes in most of his narrations.

Interest in the *récits* and soliloquies is also maintained by the alternation of new and familiar material. In the first half of II, 5, the audience learns at the same time as Arnolphe what Agnès has taken, whereas, in the second half of the scene, it is fully informed of the identity of the husband Arnolphe is proposing for his ward. In III, 4, the first part of Horace's narration of the stone-throwing incident plays back information given to the audience in II, 5; the information in the second part concerning Agnès's note comes as a partial surprise to the audience (and, of course, as a shock to Arnolphe). The soliloquy in III, 5 introduces a new element into the pattern of Arnolphe's analyses of his inner turmoil: his love for Agnès, which will become a major factor in the last two acts. In Horace's third *récit* (IV, 6), the referential element concerns not merely the past, giving a context to Arnolphe's soliloquy in IV, 1, but also his future plans (his nocturnal visit to Agnès). Horace's *récit* in V, 2 goes over familiar territory in his recounting of his fall from the ladder. The rest of his story takes by surprise both the audience on the stage and in the auditorium.

The delayed revelation of the romantic love intrigue is another dramatic device for sustaining interest and tension. The play begins with the "blocking figure", with the obstacle to the wedding of the lovers. The plot will revolve around the removal of the prospective husband, Arnolphe, and his replacement with the true lover, Horace, and concomitantly with the replacement of the guardian of Agnès by her real father. The romantic love plot is not introduced until I, 4, and the motif of real love is revealed after that of unreal love (i.e. details of Arnolphe's grand design). The unreal becomes real in III, 5 and paradoxically provides a new obstacle not only to the lovers but also to their antagonist himself. By keeping the lovers apart until V, 3, and by restricting their *tête à tête* to a brief scene, which is itself interrupted by Arnolphe's attempts to drag Agnès away (note the stage directions), Molière prolongs the young lovers' uncertainty about the outcome. Molière also keeps in focus the chief obstacle to their union, and prepares for a solution from beyond the characters' control. Finally, withholding the dénouement until the last possible moment sustains the dramatic momentum created by the exposition and development of the plot.

(B) COMIC OR TRAGIC ?

A tragic reading of the play, popular with the Romantics, has been revived in recent years (see Chapter One). Such an interpretation diverges greatly from that of Molière's contemporary critics, whose main complaint was that the play was too comic (see Chapter Six). Dorante makes a clear distinction between a tragedy and Molière's play when asserting on behalf of the author that comedy is more difficult to compose than tragedy (*La Critique*, sc. 6). Potentially serious issues are treated in the play—but in a light-hearted manner. The principal difference between *L'Ecole des femmes* and some of the tragedies with which it has been compared lies in the "angle of perception". The audience views the plight of the tragic hero from inside the character. That of the comic hero is viewed from outside. In tragedy, the response is essentially emotional: a bond of sympathy is established between character and spectator. In comedy, the response is primarily intellectual: a notional distance is created between the two parties. The degradation of Arnolphe generated laughter in Molière's audience; suffering experienced by some Racinian characters evoked pity and fear. Fixity in Arnolphe could be regarded as one of the hallmarks of the comic hero; fixity in some of Corneille's characters is, on the contrary, to be admired. In this section, I shall analyse the devices of structure used by Molière to create detachment and the angle of perception appropriate to the realm of comedy.

(i)   Stock   Elements

The setting and the type of plot indicate quite clearly that the play belongs to the comic *genre* . The outdoor location, the traditional setting for comedy and farce, is ironic in view of the emphasis on secrecy throughout the play and is in keeping with the highly improbable scheme of Arnolphe (see next section). Marriage against the inclinations of the young lovers is a topos of comic plot construction stretching back to Terence and Plautus. The series of coincidences situates the play in a world of fantasy in which we are led to expect the unexpected: the return of a father after 'mille périls divers' to recover a long-lost daughter, who turns out to be none other than Arnolphe's ward and Chrysalde's niece; an arranged marriage which mirrors the inclinations of the young lovers, and which resolves all the plot complications. In this framework, the happy ending is never in doubt for the audience; the main interest is in the way in which it will be brought about. In this respect, the comic plot differs significantly from that of tragedy. In comedy, suspense and tension are experienced mainly by the characters. The audience's detachment, and its sense of its own superiority, afford it comic perception of the characters' responses to what is for them a serious situation. In Molière's play, the audience's superior position gives comic lighting even to critical moments in the lovers' experience.

(ii) *Quiproquo*

The comic plot of *L'Ecole des femmes* rests on a triple *quiproquo* (a situation arising out of a misunderstanding): the dual name of Arnolphe; his two houses; and the true identity of Agnès. The successive revelations by Horace to the very person from whom they should have been kept depend on Arnolphe's new civil status (his recent change of name to Monsieur de la Souche) and on his possessing two dwellings. Arnolphe's upbringing of Agnès and his marriage plans are made in ignorance of her true identity. The triple *quiproquo* gives a ludic form to the play in keeping with the playful discoveries at the end.

Within the central *quiproquos*, Molière creates consequential misunderstandings which maintain the ironic rhythm—build-up / knock-down—of the play. Act II, scene 5 is constructed around a double *quiproquo*. In the first, the comic disproportion between cause and effect reaches a climax in Agnès's reiteration of the equivocal *le*. The suspension points after each one-line speech reveal the paroxysm of fear experienced by both characters. Our expectations—and indeed, those of the characters—are let down by Agnès's ultimate disclosure regarding the innocent loss of the 'ruban'. The *quiproquo* shows the comic contrast between Arnolphe's crude, street-wise cynicism and sensuality and Agnès's transparency and ingenuousness. The second *quiproquo* depends on the fact that Arnolphe had not made clear to Agnès that *he* was the intended husband. Molière protracts the misunderstanding with two new elements: Agnès's joy and Arnolphe's satisfaction; the announcement of the wedding date. Once again, the *quiproquo* is ended by Agnès. Her unwitting use of the pronoun *lui* (626), which announces her illusion of a marriage to Horace, bursts the bubble of euphoria inflated by the misunderstanding.

The *quiproquo* in IV, 2 is a variation on the last one. The audience is fully aware of the different contexts of which the two characters are speaking. The misunderstanding arises from the inattention of Arnolphe and the ambivalent language of the Notaire, who believes he is participating in a dialogue. Arnolphe's questions and reflections on how to keep Agnès and to safeguard his reputation are met with legal answers which, in themselves, form a coherent conversation. In fact, as McBride has observed (*26*, p. 12), the *quiproquo* 'is nothing less than a *reductio ad absurdum* of conversation and language, in which words can simultaneously be seen to form sense and nonsense'.

(iii) Reversal and Repetition

The idea of the robber robbed, the cheat cheated, the villain who is the victim of his own villainy, is a constant of the comic structure. In each case, the comic effect derives from the incongruity of a situation which recoils on the head of its author. When the principle of reversal is repeated, the comic effect is doubled. Repetition in itself arouses certain expectations in the spectator, the fulfilment of which gives rise to comedy. The repeated reversals in the play gives a mechanical aspect to the structure. The mechanical-seeming nature of the repetition underlines the sense of unreality, abstracting the dramatic situation from that of everyday life, in which such repeated occurrences do not (usually) take place (see Bergson).

The pattern of reversals in *L'Ecole des femmes* gives comic emphasis to Arnolphe's downfall. I shall examine those which arise from his encounters with Horace, the servants, Agnès and Chrysalde. (Arnolphe's self-contradiction will be dealt with in Chapters Three to Five).

Arnolphe—Horace

Arnolphe's first meeting with Horace in I, 4 exposes the hollowness of his imagined triumphs over his interlocutors in the first three scenes. The confident tone displayed in Arnolphe's effusive greeting and enthusiastic interrogation of Horace in the first half of I, 4 is abruptly transformed by Horace's switch from general to particular (317). In III, 4 it is again a tale of two halves: the first half of the scene leaves Arnolphe exhilarated, the second half deceives not only his expectations in the first half, but his pretensions in the first three scenes of Act III, typified in the jubilant affirmation of his success in the opening line: 'Oui, tout a bien été, ma joie est sans pareille'. Horace's reading of Agnès's letter and his invitation to Arnolphe to admire her natural simplicity (III, 4) inversely parallel Arnolphe's forcing Agnès to listen to his sermon and to recite his *maximes* (III, 2). A further comic irony is created between Horace's admiration for Agnès's 'simplicity' and Arnolphe's endeavours to keep her 'simple'. The third encounter deals a double blow to Arnolphe's hopes: Horace's account of Arnolphe's ill-tempered off-stage encounter with Agnès (which took place between Acts III and IV) rekindles the rage Arnolphe had experienced in IV, 1, but to which, this time, he cannot give audible expression until the next scene; Horace's announcement of his future plan invalidates Arnolphe's latest expression of confidence in the previous scene:

> Enfin j'ai vu le monde, et j'en sais les finesses.
> Il faudra que mon homme ait de grandes adresses
> Si message ou poulet de sa part peut entrer. (1140-42)

The first three encounters with Horace expose as illusory what Arnolphe conceives to be real. The fourth (V, 2) contradicts Arnolphe's expectations yet again, but in a paradoxical reversal of the set pattern (see Myrna Zwillenberg, p. 302). Horace's appearance leads not, like his first three entrances, to Arnolphe's humiliation, but to relief (at the news that Horace has not been murdered by the servants) and to joy (at his being asked to conceal Agnès from Monsieur de la Souche.) The illusion of triumph (and continued reversal of the pattern of reversals) is sustained in the fifth and final encounter with Horace (V, 6), in the latter's disclosure of the arranged marriage and in Arnolphe's feigned declaration of support of Horace against his father. The build-up of Arnolphe's confidence makes the final reversal at the end of the play all the more spectacular.

Arnolphe—Alain / Georgette

The exchanges with the servants, like the encounters with Horace, force Arnolphe to face reality and reveal to the audience—if not to the character—the fantasy world he inhabits. Horace's *récits* expose as false Arnolphe's perceptions of the immediate past. The servants' buffoonery renders ineffectual Arnolphe's future plans. The master's failure to control the unsophisticated servants in I, 2 offers an ironic portent of his failure to control Agnès, given Arnolphe's equation of their native simplicity and Agnès's 'bonté naturelle' : 'Et pour ne point gâter sa bonté naturelle, / Je n'y tiens que des gens tout aussi simples qu'elle' (147-48). His inability to cope with a practical problem—that of getting into his own house—deflates the confidence he had exuded in I, 1 in extolling his *précautions* . The "practical problem" has moral implications: those of the "master" kept out of his own house by his servants. Not only is his authority not accepted, but he is openly mocked in the thrice-repeated stage business with Alain's hat (a farcical demonstration of lack of respect). Arnolphe's threats of starvation, in themselves disproportionate to the servants' offence of sluggishness, and revelatory of Arnolphe's choleric temper, prove counterproductive, causing further delay: the servants vie with each other to open the door. Act I, scene 2 traces Arnolphe's comic failure: his initial expectations of a warm reception ('On aura, que je pense, / Grande joie à me voir après dix jours d' absence') are ironically fulfilled in his receiving on his own back blows which the servants had supposedly intended for each other.

In II, 2, Arnolphe's anger, vulgar expression, and incoherent orders (note the use of suspension points) contrast with his heroic depiction of his ten-day absence in the previous scene: 'Eloignement fatal! Voyage malheureux!' (385).

The revelation that Arnolphe has paradoxically been financing his own ruination—perhaps with money which is not the correct weight: 'il [Horace] nous a l'autre fois / Donné deux écus d'or qui n'étaient pas de poids' (670)— further deflates his over-confidence at the beginning of Act III. Like the *contretemps* in I, 2, the discovery of Horace's bribery anticipates the major reversal of the act in III, 4.

The rehearsal of the scenario devised by Arnolphe in IV, 3-4 to block Horace's attempts to enter the house recalls the theatrical humiliation Arnolphe had experienced with Horace. Arnolphe had assumed the status of an audience of comedy without knowing the full script; the second part of each of Horace's *récits* in I, 4 and III, 4 portray Arnolphe as the comic victim, an ending the latter apprehends as tragic. Arnolphe's failure as audience to Horace is compounded by his failure as an actor. His impersonation of Horace in IV, 4 leads to verbal, material and physical discomfiture. The servants who take their part too literally (being unwilling to distinguish between Arnolphe's performance and the real thing) insult Arnolphe, shove him, and take his money.

The bungled rehearsal gives the lie to Arnolphe's optimism in the following scene (IV, 5) and anticipates the servants' clumsy execution of the master's revised orders at the end of the act. The instruction to beat Horace (the attempted beating takes place off-stage between Acts IV and V) betrays a violence which contradicts Arnolphe's claim to *sagesse* in I, 1. Ideological discussion has given way to brute force. Ironically, even Arnolphe's naked aggression is clothed in moralising: 'Voilà pour le prochain une leçon utile' (1348). This confidence evaporates in V, 1 into panic-stricken questions and frantic attempts at self-exoneration. (Note the unconscious irony: Horace's fall was due to his own lack of agility and not to blows from the servants.) The series of reversals involving the servants reveals Arnolphe's naïveté and the impracticability of his scheme.

Arnolphe—Agnès

The reversals suffered at the hands of Agnès give further evidence of Arnolphe's mental blindness. Arnolphe's brash challenge to an imaginary audience (244-48) is based on Agnès having conformed to two of his precepts laid down in 102 ('coudre et filer')—her obedience to the other two ('Prier Dieu, m'aimer') is taken for granted. However, the sexual innuendo suggested by 'puces' (see Hall, p. 94) alerts the audience to unconscious irony in Agnès's preoccupation with 'cornettes' and 'coiffes' headgear (cf. the practice of women placing a hat on the head of cuckolded husbands). In II, 5 the double *quiproquo* and the transition both from Arnolphe's banal overtures regarding the weather to his frenetic expletives, and from

Arnolphe's wheedling enquiry about recent happenings to his abrupt dismissal of Agnès to her room: 'C'est assez. / Je suis maître, je parle: allez, obéissez', show the illusory nature of Arnolphe's authority.

Arnolphe's failure to elicit information from Agnès in III, 2 leads to further embarrassment in III, 4. Her absence from Act IV prepares the climactic reversal in V, 4 which will be analysed in Chapter 5.

Arnolphe—Chrysalde

The three meetings between Arnolphe and Chrysalde (I, 1, IV, 8, V, 7-9) are seemingly less significant than the conflictual situations examined above. Yet one of them contains the most spectacular reversal of the play (V, 7-9). The first encounter will be examined in detail in Chapter 5. The second encounter in IV, 8 parallels inversely their first, of which it is a consequence (the supper invitation). Their last meeting sees the fulfilment of Chrysalde's prediction (in I, 1) of Arnolphe's discomfiture. Arnolphe's brief, anguished interjection 'Oh!', after which he exits, is a far cry from his lengthy justification of his confidence in I, 1.

The repeated pattern of reversals, which undermines Arnolphe's plans, highlights the air of fantasy conveyed by Arnolphe's initial *exposé*. It brings us constantly back to the starting point. The comic mechanism gives ironic emphasis to the main character's mental rigidity: the arch-systematiser is himself systematically deflated.

(C) COHERENT OR LOOSELY CONSTRUCTED ?

A third criticism of the construction of *L'Ecole des Femmes* concerns its supposed lack of unity: the play has been judged to be a collection of loosely related scenes. Admittedly, it does not have the same degree of causality as a tragedy. But this is less a defect than a reflection of the more open form of the structure of a comedy. It has often been pointed out that comedy and coherence are uneasy bedfellows, since the former thrives on the incongruous, on the interruption of familiar patterns. The comic plot is built on what Moore has felicitously termed "suffusion"—one episode after another illustrating the central theme—rather than on linear development. The central focus is not on the resolution of the love plot but on Arnolphe's obsessive fear of cuckoldry. Viewed in this light, the play can be considered a unified spectacle. I shall examine ways in which coherence is achieved.

(i) The Unities

The three unities, an important feature of tragedy, were not considered essential in comedy. However, in *L'Ecole des femmes*, Molière respects all three unities—though in a way which requires considerable suspension of disbelief. Molière is not depicting life as it really is, but an illusion of life: within that illusion, there is unity.

Unity of Time

The events of the play are completed within one revolution of the sun (24 hours): 'dans [= dès] demain' (2). The play begins early in the morning with Arnolphe's return and his meeting with Chrysalde, and it ends at about the same time the next morning. Act V begins in darkness, but the day dawns progressively. Note the references to time: 'le jour s'en va paraître' (1362); 'Vous sortez bien matin' (1370); 'il fait un peu jour' (1447); 'le jour me chasse' (1477); 'Cet Enrique, dont hier je m'informais à vous' (1634). The lighting in Act V reflects metaphorically the perceptions of the characters on the stage, in particular the transition from ignorance to enlightenment through the double recognition at the end of the play.

Molière's observance of the unity of time makes for an extraordinary compression of events, which was perfectly acceptable within the comic tradition: a day in the life of Arnolphe features three meetings with his friend Chrysalde, five accidental encounters with Horace, a stroll in the garden with Agnès, the delivery of a sermon and the listening to a recital of the *maximes*, the supervision of the stone-throwing, a proposal of marriage, the summoning and dismissal of a lawyer, numerous bouts with the servants, and the reception of an old friend.

Unity of Place

In the first half of the century, there was an evolution from the *décor simultané* (different compartments on stage indicating different settings) to the *décor unique*, the single set. One may note, for example, the development in Corneille's staging: *Le Cid* (1637) has four changes of scenery (I, 1—Chimène's 'appartement'; I, 2—the Infante's 'appartement'; I, 3—the 'place publique'; II, 6—the 'salle du palais' ; *Horace* (1639-40) has a single set—le Vieil Horace's house. In *L'Ecole des femmes*, the stage represents the public square of a large town or city ('la scène est dans une place de ville' is the only indication given in the first edition). Two houses are mentioned in I, 1: the one in which Agnès is lodged (145-46), and the one Arnolphe seeks unsuccessfully to enter in I, 2; the other dwelling is presumably in the centre of the busy, commercial part of the town (143-44).

The single set has attracted much criticism: the public square is an inappropriate backcloth against which intimate confidences are shared, proposals of marriage delivered, and a legal contract is drawn up. The servants are brought outside to listen to instructions. Agnès, who has hitherto been concealed from the neighbours and passers-by, is taken outdoors to listen to Arnolphe's sermon. One of Molière's rivals, de Visé, commented on the volume of carriage traffic in the streets in the neighbourhood of Paris. De Visé was, however, expecting more realism than was either intended or required in comedy—there is no particular textual or historical evidence for situating the play in Paris, as most editors have done following the editorial accretion in the 1734 edition. Corneille in his third *Discours* (*Writings on the Theatre*, ed. Barnwell, Oxford, 1965, pp. 78-79) had already attempted to reconcile the theoretical need for unity with the psychological need for diversity of place. Corneille's idea of the 'lieu composite' is given an ironic dimension in *L'Ecole des femmes* : Molière anticipates mockingly the strain on the spectator's credulity:

> Et je la fais venir en ce lieu tout exprès,
> Sous prétexte d'y faire un tour de promenade [...]
> La place m'est heureuse à vous y rencontrer [...]
> Mais ces lieux et cela ne s'accommodent guères
> Allons dans la maison débrouiller ces mystères.
> (454-55; 1143; 1776-77)

The incongruous setting further exposes the folly of Arnolphe's plan and prepares for his public humiliation.

The exterior setting was particularly appropriate to the series of chance encounters between Arnolphe and Horace ("a funny thing happened on the way to the public square"). The house itself is given comic symbolism: the door and the window, in particular, can be perceived as metaphors of the ironic rhythm of the play, and reflect the principle of inversion: the captor / captive. As has been suggested by Nicolich, the door is closed to the master but has inadvertently been left open to Horace, during Arnolphe's absence. Arnolphe attempts to seal off this entrance (note his inner rejoicing at Horace's discomfiture in finding the door slammed in his face by the servants (633-34; 871-72)) but paradoxically opens up another channel of communication: the window (cf. the letter attached to the stone). Arnolphe's badly-executed plan to close off this exit (following Horace's confidences in 1173-75) succeeds in opening the door through which Agnès momentarily escapes (V, 2). The closure of the door transfers the potential escape route to the window (1707-1709). Entrance to the house at the end of the play is doubly ironic: Arnolphe seeks to barricade himself in the very place in which he had locked up his ward; the house will not provide a sanctuary from the outside world, or in particular, from the street: Chrysalde will lead in the company to celebrate the wedding: 'Allons dans la maison débrouiller ces mystères, / Payer à notre ami [=Arnolphe] ces soins officieux' (1777-78).

Unity of Action

The plot is unified by means of the symmetrical arrangement of the *récits* and soliloquies in Acts I, III and IV. The triple repetition charts the progress of the young lovers and the critical phases in Arnolphe's downfall (see Conesa, *36*):

> 1) The three soliloquies by Arnolphe which immediately precede Horace's *récits* plot the ascendant curve of Arnolphe's expectations. A triumphant challenge is sounded in I, 3, 244-48; the apex of the curve is reached in III, 3, the longest of his soliloquies, which marks the centre of the play; the shorter, eleven-line soliloquy in IV, 5 reveals much less self-confidence and self-satisfaction.
> 2) Intersecting the ascendant curve are the three *récits* by Horace (I, 4; III, 4; IV, 6). In the first two, Arnolphe intervenes frequently; in the last, he is silent.
> 3) The three soliloquies which immediately follow Horace's *récits* (I, 4, 357-70; III, 5; IV, 7) depict Arnolphe as dejected and dispirited, trying to bolster his deflated ego, and to devise a solution to his predicament. These soliloquies reflect inversely those which had preceded Horace's *récits* .

In the remaining two acts, in which the pattern is varied, the focus is on Arnolphe's jealousy and on the declaration of his intention to marry Agnès. In the only two scenes in which he is not visible to the audience (he is not on stage in II, 3 and is in the wings in V, 3), his jealousy is conveyed hypothetically, by Alain's comparisons between a woman and a bowl of soup in II, 3, and in reality by his cutting short the love scene between Horace and Agnès in V, 3. Arnolphe's two declarations reveal his comic degradation: from the authoritative announcement in II, 5 to the submissive appeal for Agnès's affection in V, 4. The imposed marriage at the end of the play reverses the one threatened in II, 5.

The symmetrical development enhances the ludic atmosphere of *L'Ecole des femmes*, underlined by Molière in *La Critique* : '... ce qui me paraît assez plaisant, c'est qu'un homme qui a de l'esprit, et qui est averti de tout par une innocente [...] et par un étourdi [...] ne puisse avec cela éviter ce qui lui arrive' (sc. 6).

(ii) The Dénouement

The resolution of the plot by means of two characters who are not central to its development, Enrique and Oronte, has been dismissed as an arbitrary appendage. The ending is, however, well-prepared and is coherent structurally, thematically, and linguistically (see chapter 4); it marks the final reversal of a series of reversals. Arnolphe is humiliated at the very moment he feels most secure. His rejoicing over the arranged marriage is silenced by the unfolding of the details. Seeming triumph is transformed into inglorious defeat, made all the more ironic by Arnolphe's approval of the marriage, and reneging on the promise of support given to Horace in V, 6. The final recognition scene is anticipated in I, 4: a reunion with the son of an old friend brings first of all great joy, then anguish when the visitor's news is received.

The introduction of characters from outside (the *patres ex machina*) provides an ironic commentary both on the young lovers' inability to resolve their problems themselves, and on Arnolphe's repeated invocation to fate. Enrique and Oronte act as a kind of metaphor of destiny: Arnolphe is defeated by forces he has invoked in soliloquies and, in fact, in the human form which he has attributed to them (see Zwillenberg, p. 308). Chrysalde draws our attention to this in his closing remark about providentialism (1779).

The ending also acts as a counterpoint to the exposition. In both I, 1 and V, 9, it is a tale of returning "fathers": the bad guardian, Arnolphe, after a ten-day absence, returns to arrange his marriage to Agnès; the good fathers return after a longer trip (Enrique has spent 14 years in the Americas) to carry out their plan for the wedding of Agnès and Horace. The antagonism between Arnolphe and Oronte reflects the opposition between Arnolphe and his friend Chrysalde in I, 1. The *récits* by Oronte and Chrysalde parody Arnolphe's expository *récit* in which he gives details of the sequestration of Agnès from the peasant woman, and of her secret upbringing, and the proposed marriage. The *récits* in the dénouement complete the genealogy, providing the missing information concerning the first four years of Agnès's childhood; the secret marriage of her mother; the assumed names of Agnès's parents; the secret marriage arranged for her. The double narrative at the end corresponds to the double narration of the beginning of the romance between Agnès and Horace in I, 4 and II, 5. For further discussion of the ending see Chapters Four and Five.

(iii) *Liaison des scènes*

In some of Molière's early plays, the linkage between scenes and between acts was somewhat loose. In *L'Ecole des femmes*, the joins are more natural. On two occasions one act ends and the next begins with a soliloquy from Arnolphe. At the end of I, 4, Arnolphe has momentary respite, after the shock of Horace's news; in II, 1, he attempts to rationalize the situation. The link between III, 5, and IV, 1 is the discovery of Arnolphe's love for Agnès (986-87). Between the acts, there is off-stage action: Arnolphe's abortive search for Horace (I / II); the planned stone-throwing (II / III); an encounter with Agnès (III / IV); Horace's fall from the ladder (IV / V). Arnolphe's pivotal role unifies the transitions between scenes and between acts. His ordering of exits and entrances, particularly with imperatives (199; 225; 241; 415; 459; 806; 1128-29; 1347; 1360), while adding to the play's unity, reflects his self-assertiveness. The unsolicited appearances of Horace and the inopportune arrival in IV, 8 of his guest, Chrysalde, and in IV, 2 of the Notaire, whom he had sent for in III, 1, point up the ironic rhythm and degrade Arnolphe's authority.

(iv) Supernumerary roles ?

Three roles have been regarded as superfluous: the servants, the Notaire and Chrysalde. All three amplify the absurdity of Arnolphe's conception of marriage. Though the servants do not have a decisive influence on the plot in the way that some of their more cunning counterparts do (cf. Mascarille (*L'Etourdi*, *Les Précieuses ridicules*), Covielle and Nicole (*Le Bourgeois gentilhomme*), Toinette (*Le Malade imaginaire*)), they unwittingly advance the lovers' cause by their inadvertence, clumsiness and openness to bribery.

The Notaire's fruitless mission reveals the widening gap between Arnolphe's expectations and reality; his remarks also reflect Arnolphe's deepest preoccupation.

De Visé's dismissal of Chrysalde as a 'personnage inutile' went unanswered by Molière. Some modern critics, though less scathing, have been equally disquieted by the role. Chrysalde has been reduced to a rather dull, colourless figure who contributes very little to the play. The fact that Chrysalde is absent from I, 1, to IV, 8 is explained by the necessary development of the intrigue: three meetings with Horace, two lengthy *tête à tête* with Agnès, slapstick scenes with the servants (McBride, 27 , p. 85). His participation at the end is justified in terms of his relationship to Agnès (uncle) and the symmetry it affords; his appearances mark decisive stages of Arnolphe's degradation. As we shall see in Chapters Four and Five, he provides a comic focus on the main character. Thus, like the servants and the Notaire, he is an integral part of the comic spectacle.

Chapter Three

The *École* Theme

The education of women was an issue of great interest in Molière's day. The moral, intellectual and social climate was very different from that prevailing in Western Europe today. Except at the *petites écoles*, there was no co-education, and there were no girls' schools. University education was available only for male students. Girls were educated mainly at home or in convents. Their studies were usually concentrated around practical subjects.

The legal age for marriage was twelve. There were notable examples of young brides: Mlle Bernard aged eleven; Mlle de Rambouillet and Mlle de Vauban both aged twelve. Marriages were frequently arranged; fathers could—and did—send rebellious daughters to the convent. The abuse of parental power was often condemned in moral treatises and in sermons.

The intellectual debate regarding the education of women had gathered momentum in 1662. The *précieuse* movement which had emerged as a protest against the crudely philistine excesses of the Fronde (1648-53), as well as against the annual pregnancy requirement, had found many champions. At the same time, treatises decrying female education were being published: women were regarded by some as having insufficient moral capacity to cope with knowledge.

Molière's play is therefore rooted in the social reality. However, critics have made an unjustifiable deductive leap in attempting to deduce from this Molière's ideology. For many years, the view that *L'Ecole des femmes* was a *pièce à thèse* was critically orthodox. The play was taken by some to be an expression of Molière's support for the education of all women and for their freedom to choose their marriage partner. For others, the message was more radical: Molière was a precursor of the eighteenth-century *philosophes*, in particular d'Holbach and Diderot. My interest in this chapter is not to examine pedagogical issues as philosophical problems. Such an enquiry would raise unanswerable questions: the philosophy implicit in the play is that of the author's *persona* and not that of the author; in addition, Molière left so little personal documentation that any identification between the author and his work must remain speculative. The question which can be resolved, however, is how Molière exploited the intellectual backcloth to create comedy.

(A) THE IRONIC TITLE

Between 1661 and 1664 (see Knutson, *49*), there was a brief spate of *école* comedies: Dorimond's *L'Ecole des femmes* (1661), Molière's *L'Ecole des maris* (1661) and *L'Ecole des femmes* (1662), and Montfleury's *L'Ecole des jaloux* and *L'Ecole des filles* (published in 1664, though created earlier). There is no record of *école* comedies before 1661, nor after 1664 until the next century. Molière probably did not initiate the title form: Dorimond's play or a licentious novel entitled *L'Ecole des filles*, written possibly by Scarron and secretly published in 1655 (see Hall, p. 89), may have begun the vogue. By 1662, however, the ironic significance of the *école* title was well established. Furetière in his *Dictionnaire universel* (1690) records the facetious use of the term. In Molière's first *école* play, the ironic contrast is between the "school of the strap" and the 'école du monde' (the school of tolerance and gentleness). In *L'Ecole des femmes*, the ironic perspective of the school motif can be viewed in the various pedagogical attitudes which are either stated or implied in the play.

(B) *L'ECOLE D'ARNOLPHE*

Five aspects of incongruity underline the folly of Arnolphe's pedagogy: its extreme application; the self-centred purpose to which it is put; the parodic content; the inappropriate method; the results achieved, which are quite contrary to those intended.

1) The exaggerated application of Arnolphe's scheme aligns him with other comic heroes in Molière. Though Arnolphe has traits of the seventeenth-century *bourgeois*, his world is essentially that of the *imaginaire*, whose existence is confined to the stage and who is dominated by a single obsession. Arnolphe's excessive preoccupation with cuckoldry makes him lose touch with everyday reality. Note in this respect his disproportionate use of hyperbole and constant generalisation which reduce his argument to absurdity.

2) The objective of Arnolphe's school is a personal and not an educational one: Arnolphe's self-aggrandizement, comfort and security. Agnès is trained to become a chattel in his household, or perhaps, in line with his imagery, a domesticated animal. In his description of Agnès's upbringing, Arnolphe's stated aim is to ensure fidelity in marriage. This concept, laudable in the abstract and a social norm in the seventeenth century, is for Arnolphe merely a means to an end: to avoid being cuckolded and thereby to attain mastery over his contemporaries. Arnolphe's egocentricity is illustrated in his boasting of his experiment to Chrysalde and in his desire to show off his pupil later that day; in his lampooning of cuckolds (21-45); in his challenge to the 'femmes d'esprit' (244-48), a challenge which is issued across the footlights to the audience; and in his belief that the beating which will be given to Horace will be instructive to his peers (1348-51).

3) The content of Arnolphe's programme is a parody of the Socratic ideal. The Socratic pupil was taught that "he does not know"; Arnolphe's pupil is instructed "not to know" (see Johnson, p. 181). Socrates's scepticism with regard to the limitations of knowledge becomes in Arnolphe's school dogmatism with regard to the dangers of knowing. For Arnolphe, the pupil's (wife's) ignorance is the prerequisite of a happy marriage: the better educated the pupil, the more likely she is to cuckold her husband. Arnolphe's syllabus is therefore minimal: 'Prier Dieu, m'aimer, coudre et filer' (102). The teaching of two of the three R's, reading and

writing, is regretted (cf. in particular 946-47). Arnolphe would in fact have preferred an illiterate wife to a 'femme d'esprit'. No instruction is given in poetry: note his pride in recounting her ignorance of rhyme (96-99). There is no sex education (cf. II, 5). The religious education Agnès has received from the convent is used by Arnolphe as a buttress for his egocentric design and as a means of inhibiting her relationship with Horace. The doctrine of the 'péché mortel' is invoked to inspire remorse in Agnès for having allowed herself to be kissed (on the hand) by Horace, and for having received his words of affection with interest and enthusiasm. Arnolphe's "finishing school"—his sermon and the *maximes*—reveal a further distortion of religious argument (see Chapter Four), which corresponds to Arnolphe's misappropriation of the classics (cf. the anecdote from Plutarch 447 ff.) as well as of one of the landmarks of French literature, Rabelais's *Tiers Livre* (see Chapter Five). Arnolphe's educational programme is essentially negative and has been termed 'abêtissement méthodique' (Albanese, p. 116). The *maximes* become a list of prohibitions: the wife will belong to the husband as a kind of proprietorial right; will dress solely for him—even if this means that others find her ugly; will use no make-up; will hide her eyes beneath her headwear; will accept presents from no man; will not do any writing; will avoid all social gatherings; will not gamble; will not go out on walks or picnics. A more inappropriate regimen is difficult to imagine! Arnolphe's educational programme befits an antisocial hermit and not a marriage partner.

4) The method of "rote learning" caricatured in Arnolphe's application: 'Et vous devez du cœur dévorer ces leçons' (730) was of topical interest in the seventeenth century (as it is still today!). The debate centred on the division between the traditional method of instruction and what we would now call the "direct method". Traditionalists favoured a more formal, theoretical approach in which knowledge was imparted to the pupil, while disciples of Montaigne's *De l'Institution des enfants* (composed between 1572-88) advocated a more child-orientated system.The comic effect in Arnolphe's school is derived not from the "method" he adopts but the madness of its misapplication to the realm of the emotions. He would have

done well to heed Montaigne's celebrated maxim: 'Fâcheuse suffisance qu'une suffisance pure livresque'. Not only does Arnolphe misappropriate the rote method, but he misreads the context when he adopts the doctoral tone of the theologian in III, 2. His solemn, pompous, not to say ponderous delivery of an open-air sermon is wasted on his congregation of one. His hellfire tactics are also ill-suited to the innocent addressee.

5) The results from Arnolphe's school reveal the comic discrepancy between his expectations and Agnès's attainment. They show that his programme of education was based on a misapprehension of Agnès's social origins; notwithstanding his assertion that she is of inferior peasant stock— 'vil état de pauvre villageoise'; 'monter au rang d'honorable bourgeoise'; 'le peu que vous étiez' (683; 684; 690)—Agnès, in fact, turns out to be an heiress. The successes of which Arnolphe boasts—his delight in Agnès's unawareness of basic anatomy and of the process of procreation, and his stated wish that her experience of rhyme (and of life) be limited to cream tarts—are, in fact, crass failures when examined against normative educational standards.

There is a further irony in that the very qualities which Arnolphe admires are the source of his downfall. His denial of sex education makes for his embarrassment in II, 5, when he seeks to ascertain the extent of Horace's involvement with his ward without giving away the answers. His unquestioning belief in his system and in his method precludes a more probing examination of Agnès's activities during his absence. His facile commitment to the method of rote learning delays until III, 4 the discovery that Agnès has already violated one of the *maximes* she had dutifully recited (the seventh, prohibiting writing). Had Arnolphe been more solicitous of Agnès's understanding of the *maximes*, he might have been spared further humiliation in front of Horace.

Arnolphe's revocation of his theories in V, 4 completes the discrediting of his system. His much-vaunted thesis on sexual inequality is abandoned. (Cf. 'Votre sexe n'est là que pour la dépendance: / Du côté de la barbe est la toute-puissance' with 'Tout comme tu voudras tu pourras te conduire' (699-700; 1596)). Agnès throws his lessons back at him: 'J'ai suivi vos leçons et vous m'avez prêché / Qu'il se faut marier pour ôter le péché' (1510-11). The authority of the teacher will be usurped by the pupil. The pupil awakens in the teacher inclinations which he had sought to repress in his ward. The book will give way to experience: Arnolphe will seek to learn from the school of Horace.

(C) *L'ECOLE D'HORACE*

Yet we need not lose sight of *l'école libre*. In Arnolphe's educational system, the 'maître' is Arnolphe himself (cf. 'Je suis maître, je parle: allez, obéissez' (642)), whereas in Horace's school, the preceptor is 'l'amour':

> Il le faut avouer, l'amour est un grand maître:
> Ce qu'on ne fut jamais, il nous enseigne à l'être,
> Et souvent de nos mœurs l'absolu changement
> Devient par ses leçons l'ouvrage d'un moment.
> (900-903)

Horace's eulogy of spontaneity and of pleasure contrasts with Arnolphe's insistence on repression and on duty. Horace inverts the roles that Arnolphe has created for himself and for his ward: Agnès is the captor, he is the captive, metaphorically wounded by her eyes. The theories of sexual inequality and social inferiority which underpin Arnolphe's pedagogy are parodied in Horace's deification of Agnès. Horace wants to admire Agnès, whereas Arnolphe wanted to conceal her. The instruction Horace gives to Agnès is nearer to what we would call "discovery learning", learning by imitation and by experience (cf. Agnès's *récit* of the repeated curtseys and bows (484-502)) and contrasts with Arnolphe's "talk and chalk" approach. Horace's school of gallantry is itself, however, an object of parody. Instead of the archetypal gallant, Horace is shown to be a blunderer. The would-be deliverer of Agnès has himself constantly to be rescued by her. The stone-throwing and the ladder incidents are a parody of the courtly love tradition. Agnès's window is opened not to receive Horace's gallantry, but to launch a missile in his direction. Horace's fall from the ladder makes a mockery of his romantic plan to abduct his beloved. Elsewhere, his duplicitous recourse to an *entremetteuse* to gain access to the house violates the code of chivalry to which he purports to adhere. In addition, Horace's ignorance of the true identity of his rival tutor, Arnolphe / Monsieur de la Souche, and his failure to perceive the reason for the series of coincidental encounters with Arnolphe outside the house in which Agnès has been imprisoned throw an ironical and critical light on Horace's claims regarding the sharpening effect of the tutelage of love:

> L'amour sait-il pas l'art d'aiguiser les esprits?
> Et peut-on me nier que ses flammes puissantes
> Ne fassent dans un cœur des choses étonnantes?
> (919-21)

In his mental blindness, Horace shows an unexpected resemblance to the foolish mentor he constantly decries.

(D) *L'ECOLE D'ALAIN*

The plural title suggests that the *école* theme be extended to include Georgette. Alain's school provides a further critique of Arnolphe's methods, and, in particular, of the process of argument by analogy. In III, 2, Arnolphe sets out the duties of a wife in comparison to the military, social and religious hierarchy. In II, 3, Alain anticipates the method in his ludicrous illustration of the effects of jealousy: 'Je m'en vais te bailler une comparaison, / Afin de concevoir la chose davantage'. Alain cannot explain the principle, but concentrates on the effects. His unromantic comparison between women and soup contradicts the conventional floral similes used to depict love and trivializes a potentially serious aspect of the play:

> La femme est en effet le potage de l'homme;
> Et quand un homme voit d'autres hommes parfois,
> Qui veulent dans sa soupe aller tremper leurs doigts,
> Il en montre aussitôt une colère extrême. (436-39)

(E) *L'ECOLE DE CHRYSALDE*

One cannot strictly speak as much of an '*école* de Chrysalde' as of a counselling service. Chrysalde has not been directly involved in the education of any woman in the play in the way that Arnolphe, Horace and Alain have been, though at the end, he is able to shed light on Agnès's early years. Chrysalde's attitudes have frequently been interpreted as those of the author. Apart from being impossible to prove, this hypothesis fails to examine closely the nature of Chrysalde's "counsel". Chrysalde's advocacy of a liberal education for women is excessively indulgent. His *juste milieu*, the median path between protestation and complacency is ironically an extreme in itself: 'Il y faut comme *en tout* fuir les extrémités' (1251; my emphasis). In IV, 8, Chrysalde's preaching of the "golden mean" is paradoxically as moralizing as Arnolphe's condemnation of cuckolded husbands and of liberal wives. As such, Chrysalde's views cannot be taken altogether seriously. They serve as another ironic focus on Arnolphe's *école*. .

(F) *L'ECOLE DE LA NATURE*

Finally, let us turn from the tutors or the would-be tutors to consider the chief pupil in the play, Agnès. Her naturalness and spontaneity ironically expose the unnaturalness of Arnolphe's scheme. Arnolphe had tried to impose on nature an abstract system which is life-denying. It is fitting that he should be overcome by what he sought to suppress: firstly, by Agnès's natural reciprocation of another's affection; secondly, by his own unexpected passion for his ward.

Many have discerned an evolution in the role of Agnès, and have deduced from this that Molière was proclaiming the need for a "Return to Nature". The triumph of youth over age, of the spontaneous and natural over the assumed and mechanical is, however, a stereotype of comic plot construction. Furthermore, Agnès spends relatively little time on stage and has little to say. Molière's focus is on the comic exposure of Arnolphe's false teaching.

The school of Nature, like the *écoles* of Horace and Chrysalde, is presented with ironic ambivalence. If it offers a conceptual norm for the play, it is a paradoxical one. In the final act, Agnès is not liberated by Nature (in whatever form) but, as Johnson has observed (p. 175), by a more benevolent representation of the traditional attitudes struck by Arnolphe. The enforced marriage which closes the play mirrors the one proposed at the beginning. The fact that the marriage which happens to accord with the inclinations of the lovers had been arranged long before the play begins should guard us from viewing the play as a plea for social change. If anything Molière indulges in mock didacticism in the play. In parodying the *école* of Arnolphe, he proceeds to subvert the various *écoles* (stated or implied) by which the central parody has been effected.

Chapter Four

Comic Language

Much of the criticism of the language of *L'Ecole des femmes* can be accounted for by the failure to perceive the distinctive nature of stage language. One cannot read a play as, say, a novel. The dramatist has a peculiar problem in getting speech across to the audience (particularly to the noisy seventeenth-century *parterre*). The *spectator* (unlike the *reader*) is unable to turn back in the text. Theatrical language must therefore essentially be simpler and more direct, and more forceful than ordinary speech: the *spectator* can *hear* it, only once, and it must perform its functions by characterising the speaker and advancing the action, and be seen to do so immediately. What often seems crude to the *reader* is essential to the *spectator* .

This "crudeness" is part only of the immediate impact made by the play. Beneath it lies great subtlety, and in order to appreciate this, we, like the producer and actor, must *study* the text and try to see it in terms of a performance aimed at expressing as much of Molière's comic richness as possible.

The comedy of language will be assessed in relation to the central illusion. The comic structure, we have seen in Chapter Two, depends on the central *quiproquo* and focuses on problems of identity, in particular on elements of disguise. In one sense, all theatre is based on disguise. An actor temporarily abandons his normal dress and form of speech to take on a new identity. The actor may also be required to perform a multiplicity of roles within the character he is impersonating; such roles may call forth different styles. In this chapter, Molière's use of role-playing will be examined, in particular his exploitation of language as a form of dress.

The language of all the characters will be analysed in terms of their ability, or failure, to dress up verbally. A hierarchy of roles will be established, according to theatrical criteria, grouping 1)—characters whose linguistic dress is inadequate: Arnolphe, Alain, Horace, and the Notaire; and 2)—those whose verbal costume is more appropriate: Georgette, Agnès, Chrysalde, Enrique and Oronte. (The illuminating work of Moore and Barnwell has charted the territory to be explored, and a fuller discussion of the problem may be found in 54).

(A) HAM ACTORS

Arnolphe

One of the crucial questions when dealing with Arnolphe is the means by which we are made aware of his verbal dressing-up: without that awareness, like so many modern producers, we should be unable to see the comic discrepancy between the person and the costume. Our detached, superior view of Arnolphe's posturing is secured by Molière's use of irony, the verbal inconsistencies, the inappropriateness of language to situation, the contrast and parallels between Arnolphe's expression and that of other characters, and the repetitive structural pattern (see Chapter Two) which magnifies linguistic defects to fantastic proportions and keeps us from identifying ourselves with the role-player.

At the outset, we see the incongruity between Arnolphe's many changes of verbal costume and his rabid opposition to any kind of vestimentary adornment, whether it be material or linguistic. He bans from his house all clothiers: 'Vendeuses de ruban, perruquières, coiffeuses, / Faiseuses de mouchoirs, gantières, revendeuses' (1136-37), whom he regards as accomplices of cuckolding wives. He wears dark, austere, outmoded bourgeois attire. He dresses Agnès in the plainest of 'hardes' (1159), prohibits the use of cosmetics: 'Ces eaux, ces blancs, ces pommades, / Et mille ingrédients qui font des teints fleuris' (761-62), and forbids his servant Georgette to take bribes for a new dress (1118). He proscribes certain social codes: 'Laissons ce style' (287); 'Mettons donc sans façons' (852) and inveighs against the literary make-up of the *précieuses* : 'vos vers, vos romans, / Vos lettres, billets doux' (246-47) and the verbal and sartorial elegance of the *damoiseaux* : 'Ils ont de beaux canons, force rubans et plumes [...] et des propos fort doux' (652-53).

During the play, however, Arnolphe exhibits numerous verbal habits, five of which will be examined below: those of nobleman, man of authority, *dévot* , teacher, and tragic hero. We shall see in detail how each of these ill-fitting costumes reveals the gap between what he fondly imagines himself to be and the *barbon*—old fogey—he actually is. The noble posture, the foundation garment to which all other costumes are attached, is displayed in his change of name from Arnolphe, the patron saint of cuckolds, to Monsieur de la Souche, and by his imitation of the elevated language of the *généreux* . It is exposed by the ironic associations of *souche* , his peremptory manner, his inability to sustain the high-flown style, and the materialistic nature of his vocabulary. In the first place, his ennobled title, chosen by Arnolphe for its genealogical connotations ('faire souche' in the seventeenth century signified 'être le premier d'une suite de descendants') offers a comically anticipatory illustration of his lack of success during the play. In addition to the meanings adduced by Beck: 'tree-stump' (its original meaning); 'stub'; 'shaft'; 'chimney-stack'; 'candle-stick'; 'water-pipe'; 'block-head'; 'insensitive man and fool', it signifies 'grosse bûche ou pièce de bois' or 'grosse bûche de bois propre à brûler' and is therefore more appropriate to a husbandman than to an aspirant to marriage. In the second place, Arnolphe's angry outbursts, shown in his expletives, contradict the self-control of the period's archetypal gentleman. Thirdly, Arnolphe's inflated language, conveyed in his second speech by the dignified inversion, the highly figurative 'infaillible' with its ecclesiastical overtones, and the lofty 'apanage': 'Et votre front, je crois, veut que du mariage / Les cornes soient partout l'infaillible apanage' (11-12) is punctured by the popular 'cornes' and unjustified absolute 'partout'. Finally, Arnolphe's bourgeois preoccupation with money, which above all reveals the futility of his aping the nobility, emerges in his mercantile expression of marriage: 'la chose'; 'affaires importantes' (2; 243); his use of monetary terms to convey moral obligations (384; 587; 627); his obsession with the financial disadvantages of cuckoldry—'L'un amasse du bien [...] présents à sa femme [...] l'argent qu'elle dépense [...] les gains qu'elle fait [...] . Le mari, dans ces cadeaux / Est toujours celui qui paye' (25; 28; 40; 42; 800-01); and his proprietorial attitude to Agnès, whom he regards as an investment and whose upbringing he evaluates in cost-effective terms: 'nourrie à mes dépens' (1547). Agnès's spirited rejection of such mercenary language—'[Horace] vous rendra tout jusques au dernier double' (1548)—brings home the significance of the role of money in the play and the crass materialism of the hero. Arnolphe's discomfiture invites laughter, particularly from an audience for whom nobility was considered an unmarketable commodity.

Arnolphe, posing as a man of authority (the second costume under consideration) is in practice a tyrant, whose despotism is manifested verbally in his directness, constant interruption of others, and monopolizing of the dialogue. His aggressiveness, impatience, and dogmatism, which usually signify insecurity rather than genuine authority, are emphasized in his encounters with Agnès and the servants by the inordinate number of imperatives, frequent use of verbs of volition, expressions of necessity, jussive subjunctives, and temporal adverbs, and by his tendency to enumeration. The contrast between Arnolphe's over-imperious manner and the non-compliance of the servants is a stock comic device, heightened in this play by the fact that the roles are reversed with the master being dominated by his less articulate ward and imbecilic servants (see Chapter Two). The discrediting of the authority he claims as *paterfamilias* and rebaptized aristocrat is most evident in his ludicrous use of hyperbole. See the supreme moment of unconscious irony: 'Je suffoque, et voudrais me pouvoir mettre nu' (394), his grotesque threat of self-castigation: 'Et je souffletterais mille fois mon visage' (1001), and, in particular, the grovelling declarations of love, which will be examined in Chapter Five.

I proceed thirdly to the mantle of devotion. Adjusted to that of nobleman and man of authority, this costume is comic by its inappropriateness.

Religious imagery is employed for self-protection, self-aggrandizement, and even self-deification. The vocabulary of hell, conjured up by Arnolphe as an insurance against defeat, offers an absurd illustration of the unpardonable sin: 'Vous enfiliez tout droit, sans mon instruction, / Le grand chemin d'enfer et de perdition' (649-50); 'Et qu'il est aux enfers des chaudières bouillantes / Où l'on plonge à jamais les femmes mal vivantes' (727-28). His identification of all opposition with infernal powers allows him to disclaim responsibility for any failures: the *entremetteuse* is defined as 'suppôt de Satan, exécrable damnée! [...] sorcière maudite, empoisonneuse d'âmes' (511; 535); a 'femme d'esprit' is 'un diable en intrigue' (829); *galants* are credited with diabolical powers of seduction: 'la griffe est là-dessous, / Et ce sont vrais Satans, dont la gueule altérée / De l'honneur féminin cherche à faire curée [...] les femmes sont du diable bien tentées, / Lorsqu'elles vont choisir ces têtes éventées!' (654-56; 840-41). Agnès's letter is probably devil-inspired: 'Ou le diable à son âme a soufflé cette adresse' (981); and Agnès herself is transmogrified into an endearing Lucifer: 'Malgré tous mes bienfaits former un tel dessein! / Petit serpent que j'ai réchauffé dans mon sein' (1502-1503). His inclusion of himself among the damned—'Je suffoque [...] Je souffre en damné' (394, 577)— and, ironically, the penitent—'je me mortifie' (977)—is a self-pitying dramatization of his ridiculous plight. To protect his ego and, in fact, to inspire adulation, Arnolphe usurps the prerogative of a 'directeur de conscience' (646; 649); a Mother Superior receiving the penitential vows of the novice (739-41); a law-giver (cf. the decalogue form of the *Maximes*); a creator, who fashions after the image of the rebaptized Monsieur de la Souche a new lineage invested with pre-Adamic innocence (809-11); a beneficent protector (1502-1503); and a suffering Saviour, willing to forgive her after her fall from grace (1581). The comedy lies in his singular misapplication of religious terminology to his own selfish ends, in the gradation from 'directeur de conscience' to "saviour" which invertedly parallels Arnolphe's increasing lack of success, and in the absurd combination of offices and the uncomprehending juxtaposition of Christian and pagan imagery (note his numerous apostrophes to fate).

Arnolphe's role as teacher, 'sage philosophe' (1188), or, one might even say, metalinguist, bolstered by the three parts I have just examined, takes us to the very heart of the play. The stultification of Agnès and the failure of the system he thought foolproof underline his comic misuse of pedagogical vocabulary: 'méthode' (123); 'examiner' (153); 'instruire' and 'apprendre' (which together occur thirty-three times); 'savoir' (employed no fewer than forty times—see Albanese, p.119); 'leçon sur le sujet d'Agnès'; 'maître'; 'école' (453; 642; 1497). Like Molière's doctors, Arnolphe is always talking and theorizing, never listening or observing. His theory of language, which reflects his materialistic, bourgeois attitudes, inculcates in Agnès, by means of rote learning, an unreflective tendency to parrot, leaving her ignorant of the more sophisticated verbal forms like poetry (95-98). There is the usual dichotomy between his wish to reduce Agnès's command of words to the expression of basic physical needs and his own pretentious language, larded with proverbs, literary quotations, Latinisms, archaisms, and precious expressions.

The fifth costume, the mask of the tragic hero (see Chapter Two), is donned by Arnolphe as an automatic, defensive reaction to the failure of the previous disguises. Both the disproportion of the language to the issues involved and the inconsistencies within the language secure a comic response. The grandiloquent Cornelian vocabulary is inappropriate to a trivial domestic situation. Arnolphe borrows the language of Pompée in Corneille's *Sertorius* (1867-68), first performed only ten months before Molière's play, not to send an assassin to his death, but to dismiss his dutiful ward to her chamber. The lexical and syntactical incongruities show the comic slipping of the mask as Arnolphe alternates between popular and refined speech. In the soliloquies closing the first act and opening the second, abstract, literary vocabulary and complex subjunctives: 'trouble d'esprit'; 'imprudence'; 'conter'; 'trouble'; 'ennui'; 'Eloignement fatal! Voyage malheureux!' (inappropriately employed to describe a ten-day trip into the country) clash with colloquial, mercenary expressions and direct statement: 'affaire'; 'caquet'; 'je ne suis pas homme à gober le morceau'.

The comic theatricality of Arnolphe's role is enhanced by the constant interchange between Arnolphe as spectator and performer. Through oscillations in the plot, Molière obliges the gloating spectator of the adversity of others to play the ignominious role of an amused audience to his own misfortune. A comic paradox is generated by the rebuke Arnolphe receives for not finding the spectacle of his own downfall sufficiently comic ('Et vous n'en riez pas assez' (938)). The monosyllabic utterances and hesitancy of this unwilling audience contrast with the gleeful barrage of questions and observations which had marked his self-imposed role as spectator. Further irony arises from the intrusion of Arnolphe as spectator into the heroic role he adopts in his soliloquies: the earthy vocabulary of the spectator mars the lofty tone of the tragic hero, and comically exposes the limitations of Arnolphe's acting talent.

The repeated pattern of Arnolphe's deflation, conveyed through the symmetrical nature of the plot (see Chapter Two), conditions the audience to look for holes in Arnolphe's costumes; each exposure of the real man fulfils the audience's comic expectations. An ironic perspective on the main character's folly is established on stage by Chrysalde, Horace, and the Notaire, and in *La Critique* by Uranie: 'Ma foi, je le tiens fou de toutes les manières [...] Et l'on m'en a parlé comme d'un ridicule [...] C'est un fou, n'est-ce pas? [...] Jaloux? à faire rire [...] cet homme bizarre [...] c'est un fou fieffé' (195; 331; 334; 335; 340; 1091), 'Ne voyez-vous pas que c'est un ridicule qu'il [Molière] fait parler?' (*La Critique*, sc. 6). By his unwitting mispronunciation of 'Souche' ('c'est je crois, de la Zousse, ou Souche, qu'on le nomme' (328)) Horace tears away Arnolphe's nobiliary disguise. His graphic description in IV, 6 of Arnolphe's childish tantrums further degrades the tragic *persona* which the hero had adopted in his depiction of the same incident in IV, 1. Chrysalde mocks Arnolphe's seigneurial pretensions by his implicit reminder that Souche is not far removed from Arnolphe's ungenteel origins (171-72) and gives a tug at the *imaginaire's* raiment of devotion by his ironic reference to 'tribulation' (1223). The servants' buffoonish disrespect, which highlights the dictatorial qualities of their master, emphasizes the hollowness of his authority.

Alain

Comedy also springs from the contrast and similarity between Arnolphe's verbal costumes and the language of other characters. Alain's inflated notions of his contribution to knowledge provide a comic echo of the master's hubris. Like Arnolphe, the servant sets himself up as an authority on marital infidelity, and, as we have seen, does, in fact, show more perception than his master of the effects of jealousy. However, the culinary flavour of the image in which he takes particular pride (436) instead of adorning his insight, reduces it to absurd proportions and betrays his essential gluttony. His alimentary imagery ironically anticipates his master's use of 'mitonner' (1029-31) and 'mangerai' (1595) and the crude threat of the 'chaudières bouillantes' (727) into which a misbehaving Agnès will be plunged. The servant's vanity in attempting to rise above his station is ridiculed, like the master's, by his relapses into the language of his own class: 'strodagème' (211), the imperfect reproduction of a learned expression ('stratagème')—a comic mispronunciation overlooked in some early editions which adopted the correct orthography; the colloquial nature of his archaism 'bailler' (430), an expression used only by Molière's unintelligent servants and undiscerning masters; his imprecision, reflecting Arnolphe's penchant for the word 'chose' (e.g. 428; 431); and his failure to construct a sentence under pressure (222), paralleling the repeated disintegration of his master's language.

Horace

Horace's dressing-up is used not to disguise but to convey his true feelings. But in his self-portrayal as the courtly lover, knight errant, and tragic hero, he shows an inability to master the appropriate language; our perception of the slipping of the mask—in this case, on account of its being too inexpertly donned—places Horace alongside his ridiculous counterpart.

The highly rhetorical language of gallantry is carried to extremes in

Horace's eulogistic apostrophe to love, which has, he remarks with unconscious irony, begun to rend the veil of ignorance (956). The contrast between his exaggeratedly precious tone, interspersed by Arnolphe's crude asides, and his own vituperative attack on the *barbon*, when he loses his usual composure: 'ce franc animal, / Ce traître, ce bourreau, ce faquin, ce brutal' (958-59), shows both characters in an absurd light. Indeed, Horace's metaphysical images: 'miracle'; 'tendresse innocente'; 'De la manière enfin que la pure nature / Exprime de l'amour la première blessure'; 'Un plus beau naturel peut-il se faire voir?' (910; 943; 944-45; 951), which situate his love in a cosmic perspective by placing it on the same plane as the fall of humanity, correspond to the infernal vision and recreative mission of Arnolphe. This imagery covers a rather materialistic attitude elsewhere, not dissimilar to that of the bourgeois, in his transference of the epithet 'doux' to money: '[...] l'argent est la clef de tous les grands ressorts, / [...] ce doux métal qui frappe tant de têtes, / En amour, comme en guerre, avance les conquêtes' (346-48). The comic unsuitability of his lover's costume is most obvious in his inability to conceal his love from his rival and communicate it to his lady, who takes literally the metaphors of love, thinking of physical wounds she may have inflicted by letting something fall on Horace (512-20).

His chivalric dramatization of his exploits in rescuing the damsel in distress (V, 2) is inverted by the reality of the situation—his falling from the ladder. Furthermore, the elevated expressions ('peine'; 'assignation'; 'le profond silence'; 'en querellant le sort'; 'la nuit obscure'; 'trépassée'; 'devers'; 'ce trouble'; 'transport'; 'destin'; 'fâcheux périls'; 'des appas dignes d'un autre sort'; 'des charmes si doux'; 'en faveur de mes feux') tumble out with prosaic terminology ('vingt coups de bâton'; 'ces gens-là'; 'assommé'; 'fou') and reflect his lack of physical agility.

The tragic hero in V, 6 is present only in the *jeune premier*'s imagination. The abstractions ('accablé de douleur'; 'a conclu mon malheur'; 'trait fatal') and periphrasis ('en ces lieux'), which in other contexts might arouse pity and fear, form a comic juxtaposition with the more earthy expressions ('pris le frais'; 'mettant pied à terre'; 'ruine'—a melodramatic form of 'perte'). This misuse of the jargon of *préciosité* recalls the half-baked ideas of Cathos and Magdelon (*Les Précieuses ridicules*), whose verbal cosmetics are presented in a ridiculous light.

The *Notaire*

The legal mask of the Notaire, which, unlike other costumes, is indistinguishable from the character who wears it, is comic by virtue of its irrelevance and abstraction from reality. His verbal costume in IV, 2, comprising thirty-eight expressions from legal jargon, is incoherent and unintelligible to Arnolphe, who is unaware of his presence and whose domestic situation has altered so radically since the Notaire was sent for as to render such discourse both unnecessary and undesirable. This accumulation of juridical words dehumanizes the character and makes him sound like a talking legal document. His refusal or inability to abandon the costume when talking to the servants in IV, 3 (see his use of the archaic 'quérir' and the exclamatory 'fou fieffé') shows the automatic nature of his language and his resemblance to Molière's doctor figures. His appearance is not gratuitous (see ChapterTwo); his preoccupation with legal formulae, motivated by an attempt to prevent contradiction and achieve superiority, mirrors the vanity, self-absorption, and comic obsession of Arnolphe.

(B)   ACCOMPLISHED PERFORMERS

Georgette

Georgette forms a link between the two groups in her awareness of verbally dressing up sentiments she does not feel—for example, those of dutiful servant. She wraps herself in a garb of idiocy to camouflage from Arnolphe her disrespectful behaviour and to protect herself from any punishment that it might attract. The looseness of her syntax allows for ironic ambiguities: see her apparently ingenuous comparison between her master and a mule, an image which calls to mind his asinine obtuseness and stubbornness throughout the play: 'Et nous n'oyions jamais passer devant chez nous / Cheval, âne ou mulet, qu'elle ne prît pour vous' (229-30). Her ability to manipulate dialectal forms and misconstruct sentences to her own advantage distinguishes her from her slow-witted counterpart, Alain, and matches, in a lower farcical register, Agnès's verbal superiority over Horace.

Agnès

The linguistic development of Agnès was admirably illustrated by Madeleine Ozeray in Louis Jouvet's production of 1936 at the Athénée (see Magne). Unlike other characters, Agnès does not seek to dress up but rather to break free from the mental and verbal shackles of Arnolphe. Comedy is generated by the discrepancy between the walky-talky-doll image that Arnolphe has forced her to play and the "naturally" lively and life-giving young woman she proves to be, and also by the way in which the ineffectualness of her language training recoils against her educator. The rudimentary linguistic features of the enforced role—concrete vocabulary associated with trivial domestic interests, simple narrative style devoid of irony and ambiguity, lack of selection of details, verbatim reporting and repetitiveness—cause the puppeteer responsible for them prolonged discomfort in II, 5, and force him to abandon temporarily his various roles and imitate the structures of language of his pupil.

The "natural" language of Agnès finds its apogee in the letter. The letter contains none of the conventional lovers' jargon but is extremely simple, straightforward, even naïve, not just in what it says, but in the direct way it says it. The threat of death is literally intended, and not a conceit. A parody of the courtly ideal is suggested by her unprecious, uninhibited emotional appeal. This is reinforced by the inversion of roles, with Agnès writing to an idealised lover who turns out in reality to be little more than an indiscreet flounderer. Her expression of love contrasts comically with Horace's verbal ineptitude and with the rote-learned formulas of Arnolphe (which will be analysed in Chapter Five).

Agnès's letter consists of two paragraphs, each containing four sentences, 'with each progressively lengthening in qualitative and quantitative effect' (Nelson, p. 122), and each final clause beginning with 'et'. The eight-fold repetition of the conjunction 'et' anticipates the eight rhyming couplets introduced by 'et' in the dénouement. This stylistic feature amplifies the paradoxical presentation of the genuine article. Agnès uses the conjunction to develop her account of the real awakening of love. In the last scene of the play, 'et' is used to give continuity to the disclosure of identities, the uncovering of falsehood, and the sealing of the lovers' union. By its rhythmic parallelism Agnès's epistolary style approximates, in a more limited form, to the verbal choreography of the ending. Despite Agnès's philistinism, and though the letter is not of great literary merit, it approaches the highly artistic medium of ballet.

Enrique

The consistently high register of Enrique's language reveals contrapuntally the inadequacy of the instruction which Arnolphe has given to his daughter, and the level which she might have attained had she not been separated from her father and brought up by her guardian. He has enriched himself linguistically as well as materially in his fourteen years in the Americas (267-71), and this highlights the gap between accumulation of liquid wealth and verbal aridity in Arnolphe. Enrique's role may therefore be regarded as more than that of an unsatisfying dramatic utility.

Chrysalde and Oronte

The verbal *pas de deux* of the dénouement, performed by Oronte and

Chrysalde, has been dismissed as artificial and irrelevant. On stage, their lines have frequently been cut, and in one notable production music was played to disguise the seeming "feebleness" of the script. Study of the form of language used by Oronte and Chrysalde reinforces, however, the conclusions drawn in Chapter Two regarding the structural and thematic unity of the ending. Given Arnolphe's assumed idiom and the unnaturalness of his scheme, the most unnatural outcome serves poetic justice. The sustained harmonious verbal fantasia makes Arnolphe's speechless onomatopoeic interjection, 'Oh!' (1764) the only discordant note and offers a retrospectively ironic comment on his inability to imitate correctly the high-flown utterance which he deems appropriate to the role of Monsieur de la Souche. The linguistic isolation of Arnolphe by Chrysalde and Oronte is the most logical and comically fulfilling conclusion. For, throughout the play, and particularly in his soliloquies, Arnolphe has cut himself off from the rest of humanity by his dressing up, out of the desire to distinguish himself from others and to avoid being laughed at. The only distinction achieved, however, is that of the chief victim of a farce, whose status is much lower than that of the average man. In fact, Arnolphe's parting exclamation is more empty than the mechanical usage of his ward and more incoherent than the disjointed protestations of his servant Alain. It demonstrates the mental and emotional instability of a little boy and contradicts his physical age and earlier claim to maturity (1188).

The rhyming couplets also highlight Horace's gauche manipulation of abstraction. The narrative mode of the couplets throws into comic focus Horace's use of the *récit* to recount his exploits. The son has no doubt imitated his father's style, given his love of dramatization and of epic and fanciful vocabulary. The difference, however, lies in the fact that his father's hyperboles—for example, 'mille périls divers' (1746)—are controlled, more appropriate to the unfortunate adventures of Agnès's parents, and not inconsistent with the rest of his language.

The couplets also set out a theatrical paradox which lies at the heart of Molière's work, and which relates the dénouement of *L'Ecole des femmes* to the masquerade of other plays by Molière: the use of artifice to expose reality. Molière clothes Oronte and Chrysalde, long-standing friends of Arnolphe and no doubt from the same social class, with very artificial and stylized diction, to remove the laudable disguise of Enrique's 'feints noms' (1742) and the pseudo-aristocratic fabric of the *imaginaire*, the character who is most out of touch with reality. Stripped of his various costumes Arnolphe has to leave the stage to seek covering for his humiliating verbal nudity—'*s'en allant tout transporté, et ne pouvant parler* '(stage direction).

Molière's use of verbal costume gives a satisfying formal cohesion to this play. It raises the problem of correct usage; as Oronte comments with unconscious irony: 'Vous ne nous parlez point comme il nous faut parler!' (1731). But Molière does not seek to impose any solution. Those who do are ridiculed: Arnolphe, for tailoring the language of his ward to the gratification of his own selfish desires and for selecting for himself the most inappropriate wardrobe; the Notaire, for his naïve belief in the all-sufficiency of his verbal gown. Neither character stays till the end of the undressing scene. The Notaire is the only absentee from the dénouement, his mask being so firmly attached that it could not be pulled off. Arnolphe, we have seen, dashes for fresh togs, once he is divested of the noble "frippery" of Monsieur de la Souche. Alain and Horace, who have tried unsuccessfully to appear more elegant, are left with a delusive image of themselves, unaware that they have failed to get inside the roles they have been playing, or even that they have been playing a role. Agnès has obtained her freedom from the tyranny of Monsieur de la Souche: nature triumphs and takes revenge on the one who sought to repress it. But lest we seek to rehabilitate a thesis rejected in Chapter Three, Agnès's letter (and to a greater extent the illusive language of Oronte and Chrysalde) suggest that the reality behind the mask is penetrated not merely by nature, but mainly by the creative, esoteric medium of verbal dance, in which words are set aside from their everyday usage. Herein lies the secret of good and bad acting.

Chapter Five

Commentaries

The commentaries are selected from the two most significant passages in the play which have not been covered in depth in the preceding chapters (Act I, scene 1 and Act V, scene 4, 1586-1611). The passages differ greatly in length and tone and will require, if not a different method, at least a differently-weighted application of the four main guidelines adopted below: (i) situation; (ii) structure; (iii) detailed analysis; (iv) conclusion. My emphasis in the first passage will be on the essential elements of the scene; the twenty-six-line extract lends itself to an almost line-by-line analysis.

****

(A)   ACT I , SCENE 1

(i)   Context

This passage forms the opening scene of the play. It is set in an unspecified large town or city described vaguely as 'ici' (22). The scene serves to introduce all the main characters except Horace, to expose the situation and the antecedents of the plot from the perspective of the two characters on the stage. Subsequent information—e..g. the fact that during Arnolphe's ten-day absence (referred to in 199-20; 465), Agnès has been courted by Horace (cf. I, 4)—will give retroactively an ironic dimension to that perspective.

(ii) Theme and Structure

The scene is constructed around four main themes: i) Arnolphe's decision to marry (1-8); ii) views on marriage and cuckoldry (9-73); iii) his grand stratagem to avoid being cuckolded—a) described generally in relation to views on the education of women (73-123), and b), specifically with regard to Agnès's upbringing (123-64); iv) Arnolphe's change of name (165-94).

The comic rhythm of the play is established in the first scene. Arnolphe's tone is assertive (2); provocative (9-12); caricatural (21-45); assured (72-80) to the point of complacency in his vulgar pleasantry (97-99); before descending to the indignant, magisterial retort (117-22), which is provoked by Chrysalde's warnings about the dangers of the ignorant and ingenuous woman (107-116). Arnolphe's narration of Agnès's upbringing restores confidence so that he again reaches a pinnacle of self-satisfaction with another coarse joke (160-64). His displeasure at not being recognized by his new title, Monsieur de la Souche is momentarily offset by his savouring ('plaît' 'appas' (174, 185)) what he believes has given him ascendancy over his friend. But the double aside which closes the scene (195-99) reveals a breakdown in communication, a *dialogue de sourds* : instead of admiration, Arnolphe's argument has provoked in his audience, Chrysalde, only fear—note the constant use of verbs of fearing—and laughter—Chrysalde's ironizing culminates in his belief that his friend is certifiable, 'fou de toutes les manières' (195).

The length of the speeches reveals Arnolphe's monomania. His constant interruption of his friend (20; 45; 73; 81; 106; 158; 165; 192) gives evidence of a self-assertiveness and an intolerance of opposition or disagreement. Absorbed by his *idée fixe* , Arnolphe turns Chrysalde's appeal for brevity (81) into a twenty-line tirade (82-102). Chrysalde's one-line retorts (123; 155; 165) show his frustration and his awareness of the futility of prolonging the argument.

(iii) Detailed Analysis

1) We are given the impression of interrupting a conversation with Chrysalde's request for clarification of Arnolphe's intention ('dites-vous'). The timetable for the wedding ('dans demain'), while satisfying the requirement of the unity of time, gives urgency to Chrysalde's attempts to dissuade his friend. The comic contrast between the two characters is immediately revealed in their formulation of the concept of marriage: Chrysalde's polite circumlocution 'lui donner la main' and Arnolphe's mercantile expression 'la chose'. One of Arnolphe's problems will be the misapplication of his business acumen to the emotions. Note his failure to take into account the girl's inclinations or even mention her until 129 (and even then, not by name). Arnolphe's first word 'Oui' alerts us to the character's self-delusion: his expression of agreement parallels yet diverges from Chrysalde's question—cf. Chrysalde's repetition of 'vous' (1), which is indicative of his surprise, and his more explicit misgivings in his second speech, culminating in his direct warning (8). The ironic force of Arnolphe's 'Oui' will be perceived at the end: the matter will be expedited 'dans demain' (though not in the way Arnolphe had expected).

2) The polarisation of the two characters increases in their general discussion of marriage and cuckoldry. Arnolphe sets himself apart from his friend (9-12), then from local husbands (21-45). His feelings of superiority over Chrysalde are communicated by the condescending mode of address: 'notre ami' (9; cf. 73), by the antithetical arrangement of pronouns 'chez vous / chez nous'; 'vous trouvez / je crois'; and by his implying, albeit in muted form (cf. 'peut-être' and 'je crois'), that Chrysalde is arguing from a position of weakness: that of a cuckold ('cornes' (12) = the traditional emblem of cuckoldry in medieval *fabliaux*). Whether Arnolphe's taunt has any foundation is a moot point (see Howarth, *3*, p. 120). His gloating over the misfortunes of cuckolded husbands (21-45) in his portrayal of six *ménages à trois* illustrates his obsessiveness and prepares the comic reversals.

Arnolphe seems to evolve a new moral hierarchy in which the loss of wealth is regarded as the second most heinous crime after cuckoldom: note the multiple references to material goods: 'amasse du bien'; 'présents'; 'gagne au jeu'; 'l'argent qu'elle dépense'; 'Sur les gains'—the husband whose wife benefits financially being deemed 'un peu plus heureux'. Reductionist argument—note the rhetorical categorizing: 'L'un [...] l'autre'—and the ironic use of ethical terminology: 'patients'; 'vertu'; 'fort honnêtement'; 'se purger'; 'rend des grâces à Dieu', betray the narrow, eccentric world view of the *imaginaire*, based on a pharisaical belief in his own rectitude and in his own invulnerability.

Chrysalde's considerable rhetorical skill (45-73) serves as a norm against which Arnolphe's stump oratory may be evaluated. The fatuousness of Arnolphe's lists, doctrinaire assertions, and categorization is demon- strated by Chrysalde's logical method of analysis. Chrysalde's objections are arranged in a nuanced pro and con argument, which shows an attempt to enter into his interlocutor's inclinations—note the use of 'mais' (15; 45; 49; 65) and 'Pourtant' (55); 'car' (17; 19; 56); 'Ainsi' (59); concessives (49; 51); attenuating adverbs 'quelque' (60), 'presque' (61), 'peut-être' (63). In 45-72 Chrysalde counters Arnolphe's concrete particularities with abstract and impersonal constructions. The uncomprehending attitude of Arnolphe, however, forces Chrysalde to make his remarks more pointed by the end of the speech.

3) (a) Arnolphe adopts Chrysalde's method of arguing to explain the reason for his confidence—his "foolproof" scheme for guaranteeing marital fidelity. The linguistic habits of the characters are momentarily exchanged: Chrysalde becomes more direct in his challenging interrogations and barbed glosses of Arnolphe's terminology: 'sotte'; 'stupide'; 'bête' (81; 103; 107-16); Arnolphe adopts the proverbial mode (74; 82; 84; 94) and uses the language appropriate to a rational discussion: 'Je sais [...] Contre [...] Je crois [...] Mais [...] Et je sais'. However, Arnolphe misapplies the objective method to a highly subjective (and ludicrous) cause: the defence of his sequestration of a four-year-old and of his keeping her in total ignorance to ensure her fidelity to himself as a marriage partner. His maxims are further subverted by the ambiguity of the word 'sot' (which means

'cuckold' as well as 'simpleton'—see Hall, p. 88). Moreover, Arnolphe is unable to sustain his impersonal stance: note the increasing use of the first person pronoun, categorical expressions, the repetition of 'je veux', the accumulation of imperatives (119-20) and the recourse to a literary authority, Rabelais.

Arnolphe's general introduction degrades his scheme even before his detailed disclosures. Negative expressions reflect an automatic defence mechanism and obsessive fear: 'pour n'être point'; 'mauvais présage'; 'un saint que pas un ne réclame'; 'Non, non, je ne veux point'. The ideal woman is presented as the antithesis of the 'femme d'esprit': without access to poetry (95-96), lacking social graces (97-99), ignorant (100), and possessing only such skills as are perceived as useful to Arnolphe (102). His vision is caricatured in his overturning, in response to Chrysalde's taunts, of two of the common requirements in a wife: beauty and intelligence—Arnolphe's stated preference is for 'une laide bien sotte'. The comic subversion of Arnolphe's value judgements is also apparent in his rationalisation of such expectations as 'l'honnêteté' (106).

3) (b) Arnolphe's *récit* giving the detailed application of his scheme (123-54) can be viewed as a parody of the traditional expository *récit* . The audience on stage is not an eager listener who is impatient to know what has happened, but an ironic, detached spectator. There is no feed line to prepare the *récit* : Chrysalde's 'Je ne vous dis plus mot' is, if anything, a conversation-stopper! In fact, Arnolphe has himself to justify the chronicle of events, by anticipating a question (149) which was probably not in the mind of his interlocutor. The narration of the events is mock-heroic. The unadorned setting parodies the ornate surroundings within which the heroine in tragedy is frequently imprisoned: 'Je l'ai mise à l'écart [...] / Dans cette autre maison, où nul ne me vient voir' (145-46). Characters introduced by the narrator reflect his *idée fixe* : servants are selected not for practical skills but on account of their ignorance; Agnès's presumed genealogy is presented from a materialistic standpoint to convey her supposedly inferior status: 'aucun bien ni naissance'. Arnolphe's base plan is portrayed as an illustrious design: note the incongruity between his

graduated self-congratulation 'ma politique [...] quels soins [...] j'ai béni le Ciel' and his overall intention: 'la rendre idiote autant qu'il se pourrait'. The acquisition of Agnès for a paltry sum and Agnès's deprived education are disguised as a mission of charity (note the value judgements: 'pauvreté pressée'; 'bonne paysanne'; 'beaucoup de plaisir'; 's'ôter cette charge'; 'Dieu merci'; 'j'ai béni le Ciel' (131-34; 139; 141)). The choice of a malleable four-year-old is elevated to the romantic status of love at first sight: 'Un air doux et posé [...] / M'inspira de l'amour pour elle dès quatre ans' (129-30); note that the word love is not mentioned again by Arnolphe until III, 5. Responsibility for the sequestration is toned down by the use of the abstract and impersonal subjects: 'Un air doux [...] il me vint la pensée'. The accumulation of twenty-nine pronouns and possessive adjectives in the first person and the emphatic description: 'Je la fis, selon ma politique [...] ordonnant' betray, in the light of future developments, not the man of authority which Arnolphe seeks to project but that of the *capitan* of the farce tradition, whose heroism is only in his imagination. The use of the perfect tense to convey the continued success of Arnolphe's scheme (139-41) will be called into question by the succession of verbs in the historic present in Agnès's account, in II, 5, of Horace's first visit: 'il me refait'; 'j'en refais'; 'j'y repars'; 'il passe, vient, repasse'; 'Me fait'.

The formal structure of the *récit* , which relates, in four chronological stages, the distant past (two phases: 129-34 and 135-38); the more recent past (143-48); and the present—note the transition from past historic to perfect to present—, is parodied by the low content and the false climax. Instead of the progressive build-up towards a climax, Arnolphe's narration ends with what is normally a preamble (the justification of the *récit*) and the rather prosaic invitation to supper. The coarse postscript (159-64), prefaced with unconscious irony: 'La vérité passe encor mon récit', serves not as a concluding proof of his scheme to create in a wife a model of innocence, but as a *reductio ad absurdum* of his attempt in 123-54 at heroic narration.

4) The new conflict centring on Arnolphe's change of name arises paradoxically from Chrysalde's attempt to avoid further disagreement with his conciliatory: 'Je me réjouis fort, Seigneur Arnolphe' (165). The new

subject is not a digression, but marks the last stage of Arnolphe's strategy to avoid being cuckolded: his wish to escape the mockery associated with Arnolphe—Saint Arnolphe, Arnolph, Arnold or Arnoul was in the medieval *fabliau* tradition the patron saint of cuckolds. The appellation also reflects Arnolphe's aspirations to nobility, though these pretensions have already been discredited by his language and behaviour. The dual name is vital for the development of the plot. Molière prepares Horace's confidences in Chrysalde's anticipation of possible misunderstandings (187-88) and in Arnolphe's stated indulgence towards the uninitiated (189-90)—i.e. Horace, in I, 4.

The folly of Arnolphe's change of name is indicated both by the associations of the word 'souche' (see Chapter Four) and by Chrysalde's ironizing, provocative question and exclamation (169-73; 175-76) and capping of Arnolphe's allusion to Rabelais with a literary topos (177-82)

(iv) Conclusion

In the portrayal of Arnolphe in this scene we see the three main hallmarks of Molière's comic heroes: obsessiveness, self-absorption and self-delusion. Arnolphe's preoccupation with cuckoldry lies at the heart of his absurd scheme. His self-assertiveness has been seen not only in the scheme itself but also in the language (first person pronouns and possessive adjectives and the uneven distribution of speeches). Arnolphe's self-delusion is apparent in the illogicality of his arguments and in his ironic aside in which he attributes his lack of success in the scene to Chrysalde's self-opinionatedness.

Arnolphe's self-delusion is also evident if the scene is situated within the general structure of the play. The failure of Arnolphe to convince his friend is a portent of future discomfiture. The announced (152) reversal of roles in their second encounter in IV, 8, where Chrysalde is assertive and Arnolphe non-committal, sheds ironic light on 155-56. The third meeting (V, 9) between the two friends completes Arnolphe's degradation and at the same time brings the audience full circle: Arnolphe's exasperated 'Oh!' (1764) follows Chrysalde's reiteration in 1761-62 of the advice given in 7-8. Chrysalde's artificial *récit* supplies Agnès's missing genealogy and the true antecedents of the action—the arranged marriage; it also exposes retrospectively the limited perceptions of Arnolphe as narrator in 123-54.

Arnolphe's confidence in the opening scene is also dented by the ensuing horseplay with the servants in I, 2, and by subsequent reversals (see Chapter Two). His appreciation of both the servants and of Agnès will turn to insults: the 'simple' servants are later called 'canaille maudite'. The expression 'bonté naturelle' in relation to Agnès will be corrupted to 'l'impudente'; 'la vilaine'; 'une bête trop indocile'.

Viewed retrospectively, the language of the passage is full of irony. Chrysalde's warnings prefigure the role of fate: 'coups de hasards' (13); 'par un sort qui tout mène' (59), and enunciate the theme of the *précaution inutile* : 'Et bien sot, ce me semble, est le soin qu'on en prend' (14); the principle of rebound: 'qui rit d'autrui / Doit craindre qu'en revanche on rie aussi de lui' (45-46); the cuckold's revenge: 'un revers de satire' (56); the inversion of roles: 'Vous devez marchez droit pour n'être point berné; [...] Gare qu'aux carrefours on ne vous tympanise' (70; 72; cf. 674).

Arnolphe's challenging declarations are contradicted by what takes place: 'Bien huppé qui pourra m'attraper sur ce point' (74)—Horace is anything but 'huppé' (='malin'); the 'mauvais présage' (84) is not the 'femme habile' but the 'sotte', as Chrysalde rightly warns (115-16)—in fact, Arnolphe will adopt Chrysalde's terminology in 1608, and we find his proud boasts of an understanding of women and of invulnerability (75-77) deflated by Agnès's ruses. His claim to far-sightedness (145) is undermined by Horace's visit (cf. I, 4 and II, 5); the categorical assertions (e.g. 'en femme, comme en tout, je veux suivre ma mode') will be revoked in V, 4 (cf. 1596).

With unconscious irony, Arnolphe predicts his own fate: 'Je serais comme un saint que pas un ne réclame' (an allusion to Saint Arnolphe), and announces his self-delusion in his jocular parenthesis confirming the veracity of Agnès's naïve utterance: 'pourrait-on se le persuader?' (161)

Another form of irony is found in Arnolphe's misapplication of religious and literary allusions: contrast his 'en bon chrétien' (83) and his belief in the providential ordering of his scheme (139; 141) with Chrysalde's closing remark regarding true providentialism (1779); Arnolphe's identification (118) with the all-wise giant, Pantagruel, rather than with the fool, Panurge, who seeks the giant's counsel on whether to get married or not. Though the immediate context of Arnolphe's citation is the question of 'debt', most of the *patrocinations* in this particular work by Rabelais are about cuckoldry.

The first scene is similar to other opening dialogues in Molière which bring together a dogmatic, intransigent character and a detached, easy-going type: cf. the brothers in *L'Ecole des maris*, the two sisters in *Les Femmes savantes* and the two friends in *Le Misanthrope*. In *L'Ecole des femmes*, the first scene forms part of the exposition, not complete until I, 4, which introduces Horace and plants the seeds of the dénouement with the announcement of the visit of Oronte and Enrique. As in other comedies by Molière (notably *Le Malade imaginaire*), the false bridegroom is introduced before the true one. The supper invitation and the fixing of the wedding set the play in motion, and the remainder of it will focus on the thwarting of Arnolphe's stratagem.

*****

(B)   ACT V , SCENE 4 , 1586-1611

(i)   Context

The extract is taken from the end of V, 4. Arnolphe and Agnès are brought together for the first time since III, 2, a scene in which Agnès was forced to read the *Maximes du mariage*. Act V, scene 4 shows the distance the two characters have travelled since their last encounter: in III, 2, the word love is never mentioned and Agnès is totally subservient. Arnolphe's passion is discovered in III, 5 and IV, 1, but is confined to soliloquies. The passage about to be studied is the climax of Arnolphe's declaration to Agnès. It follows the first *tête à tête* on stage between Horace and Agnès

(V, 3), the progress of the lovers having previously been charted in *récits*. The juxtaposition of the two love scenes invites the audience to compare both the wooing of Agnès by the two rivals and Agnès's response. The presentation of the reciprocal relationship in V, 3 provides a norm against which Arnolphe's amatory language may be assessed. This norm is expressed ironically: Horace and Agnès are obliged to declare their love not only in the presence of the chief obstacle to their wedding, but with the latter (albeit with his cloak over his head), in the archetypal lover's stock pose— holding Agnès's hand. This reversal prepares for Arnolphe's adoption of the lover's role in the passage under review.

From the dramatic standpoint, the extract occurs at a critical moment for both characters. Unwittingly handed over by Horace in V, 3 to the very guardian from whom she had at last managed to escape (V, 1-2), Agnès has discovered the identity of her would-be protector (beginning of V, 4). Arnolphe is sorely troubled by the spectacle of mutual love witnessed in the previous scene, and by the threat that this represents to his plan to marry Agnès himself. His enforced eavesdropping on Horace's intimate conversation with Agnès parallels Horace's overhearing (from a cupboard) Arnolphe's attempt at intimacy, which resulted in table-thumping, striking a dog, and breaking china (see IV, 6). Set against the pattern of reversals in the play, this parallel leads the audience to anticipate Arnolphe's failure in the passage under review; Arnolphe has repeatedly shown himself incapable of exploiting the intelligence he receives from Horace. To counteract this latest, first-hand evidence of the lover's situation, Arnolphe seeks to emulate the gallant language of Horace himself. We may compare Horace's 'flamme amoureuse' and 'mon amour extrême' with Arnolphe's variations in 1599 and 1604; here, Arnolphe adopts a form of language for which he had previously expressed his abhorrence (see 244-48). In the first part of V, 4, Arnolphe has oscillated between anger and what he calls "tendemess". Agnès's rejection of his overtures forces him to be more explicit and openly to avow his love in 1586-1604. His declaration is a response to Agnès's polite question regarding the cost of and her capacity for loving Arnolphe.

(ii) Theme and Structure

The passage reveals both the most extreme expression of Arnolphe's love for his ward and his deepest humiliation. The extract can be divided into three sections, following the speeches:

1) The symmetrical construction of Arnolphe's avowal gives comic emphasis to his failure. His confident exordial focus on Agnès's capacity for loving him (1586) is concluded by an affirmation of total self-abnegation (1604)—which is in itself self-contradictory. In between, the accumulation of imperatives to persuade Agnès to find her happiness in Arnolphe and not in Horace (1587-88) descends to a barrage of questions formulated in a mock-tragic register (1600-1603). These belie the sense of inevitability which Arnolphe has tried to convey with the series of futures (1591-96).

2) Agnès's laconic rejoinder deflates Arnolphe's rhetoric and unleashes the volte-face produced by Arnolphe's final speech in the scene.

3) The reversal of roles, from that of cajoling, wheedling lover to that of theatrical villain, is expressed in the adoption of the more formal *vous*, in the resumption of the threatening tone which had prevailed in Arnolphe's previous encounters with Agnès, and in the brevity of his remarks (Arnolphe is only too eager to terminate a discussion which had become humiliating for him). The use of the future tense and of animal imagery emphasizes the change of mood. The idyllic vision conjured up by Arnolphe's future tenses in 1591-96 is contradicted by the imperative use of the tense at the end of the scene—'vous dénicherez [...] me vengera'. Terms of endearment such as 'mon pauvre petit bec' are replaced by the vocabulary of abuse—'bête trop indocile [...] vous dénicherez'.

(iii) Detailed Analysis

1) Arnolphe's mental blindness, shown in his belief that love can be manufactured at will (1586), is illustrated by inadequate attempts to change Agnès's inclinations (in which he has been totally uninterested until now).

A farcical tone is suggested by Arnolphe's incongruous commentary on his performance as a lover. The abstract terminology, 'soupir amoureux' and 'regard mourant', is misapplied to the exaggeratedly self-conscious gestures (traditionally the sigh—see the stage direction—is drawn from the depths). As has been suggested (Hall, p. 133), Arnolphe's use of heroic language evokes the braggart soldier who 'makes a fool of himself and then calls attention to it'—see 'contemple ma personne' (1588). His focus is also not on the perfections of the lady but on his performance as a lover. In addition, Arnolphe's invitation to Agnès (1587-88) is in sharp contrast to his summons at the beginning of III, 2:

> Agnès, pour m'écouter laissez là votre ouvrage.
> Levez un peu la tête et tournez le visage.
> Là, regardez-moi là, durant cet entretien;
> Et jusqu'au moindre mot imprimez-le-vous bien.
> (675-78)

An early engraving of III, 2 shows Agnès standing in front of Arnolphe, who is sitting down and pointing to his forehead (cf. pupil-teacher relationship—also the unconscious irony in the association of the forehead and 'cornes', the traditional symbol of cuckoldry). In V, 4, Arnolphe is most probably on his knees as a suppliant. There is also comic descent in Arnolphe's disclosure of the purpose of his appeal with his fourth imperative 'quitte ce morveux'; 'morveux' devalues the more high-flown abstract terms. It is not insignificant that Horace is named not by Arnolphe but by Agnès; in seventeenth-century theatre, naming a character is often very emotive. The reference to 'sort' is doubly ironic: at one level, it reveals Arnolphe's vanity in his unwillingness to accept defeat at the hands of any ordinary mortal; at another level, it anticipates the arranged marriage at the end of the play.

Arnolphe is concerned with physical rather than psychological aspects of love (in keeping with his bourgeois materialism which depreciates the claim to nobility made in his assumption of the title Monsieur de la Souche). This is illustrated in the choice of physically expressive verbs: 'écoute'; 'vois'; 'contemple'; 'quitte'; the extravagant 'soupir' in his attempt to quantify happiness; and in his new-found belief that the way to a woman's heart is through clothing ('brave' = 'qui fait belle figure à la parure'; 'leste' < 'lesto' [Italian] = 'élégance pimpante, alerte, dégagée'). Note the comic contradiction of the second, third and fourth *maximes*, which prohibited any form of adornment, and which have led to Agnès being attired in the very plain 'hardes' (1159). The solemn connotations of 'protester' (='protester quelque chose avec serment') recall the religious framework of the *maximes*, which Arnolphe is implicitly rewriting in this scene. The law of love has become a new commandment (cf. the imperatives and futures) or a new covenant (cf. 1610 'vœux'), replacing the outmoded decalogue of III, 2 (and providing further evidence of Arnolphe's self-deification). The most extreme revocation of Arnolphe's former decrees occurs in 1596, which is glossed by a scarcely-veiled invitation to Agnès in the next line to make him a cuckold, a fate he has striven throughout the play to avoid. These two lines reverse the first, fifth, sixth and tenth *maximes* and his autocratic: 'Je suis maître, je parle: allez, obéissez' (642).

Arnolphe's portrayal of himself as the sensual lover in 1594-95 is also discredited by the inapposite 'bouchonnerai' and 'mangerai' : the equine associations of 'bouchonner' (= 'to rub down', of horses) take us back to Arnolphe's equation of women with animals in 1579: 'On fait tout pour ces animaux-là'; the term 'mangerai', which presents Agnès as a culinary delicacy, recalls images from gastronomy chosen by Arnolphe to describe domestic bliss and Alain's celebrated comparison of women with soup (cf. 97-99; 436; 1031). The accumulation of futures (1593-96) reveals the gap between illusion and reality: the conditional mood would have been more appropriate to Arnolphe's hypothesis.

The aside in 1598 has generally been considered to be a moment of lucidity. It is, paradoxically, further evidence of Arnolphe's self-deception and echoes the many soliloquies in which he has acted as an uncritical spectator of his own performance. Agnès's silence forces a change of emphasis and of role, from so-called gallant lover to tragic hero. The aside itself can be considered mock-tragic, particularly if one accepts that its immediate source is in Corneille's *L'Illusion comique* : 'Dieux! jusques où l'amour ne me fait point descendre!' (see Howarth, *3*, p. 135). The unconscious irony of 1599 recalls the self-assessment of other comic heroes in Molière, who have drawn attention to the uniqueness of their love. The tragic resonance of 1600 and 1604 is caricatured by the detailed elaboration in 1601-1603. Weeping, self-mutilation, tearing out hair and suicide were prominent features in some of the melodramatic tragedies of the 1630s; the difference here lies in Arnolphe merely threatening to perform these actions. Arnolphe's expression preserves the comic register: 'pleurer' is prosaic; 'me tue' is already a climb-down from the more lofty 'regard mourant' (1588); 'me batte' evokes the beatings of the *commedia dell'arte* and the physical aspects of the reversals in IV, 4 which arose from Arnolphe's impersonation of Horace as an unrequited lover; the over-precision 'un côté de cheveux' reduces the tragic gesture to absurdity.

2) Agnès's detached, two-sentence reply punctures Arnolphe's inflated rhetoric and contrasts with the warmth she had shown to Horace's overtures in the previous scene, which Arnolphe refers to in 1496: 'Tudieu! comme avec lui votre langue cajole!' Agnès's words in 1605-1606 offer retrospectively an ironic commentary on Arnolphe's performance: her directness and plainness of speech expose the futility of his recourse to gallant expression and to the tragic mode (note her unadorned evaluation of the two rivals: 'tous vos discours [...] Horace avec deux mots'). Her hypothesis, formulated correctly in the conditional mood, shows the inefficacy of Arnolphe's futures; the quantitative hyperbole 'deux mots' contrasts with Arnolphe's 'cent fois plus heureuse' and with his accumulation of temporal adverbs: 'toujours', 'sans cesse nuit et jour'; the focus on the psychological and the emotional: 'ne me touchent point l'âme' invalidates Arnolphe's proccupation with the material. Agnès's speech reveals a self-assurance lacking in her previous encounters with Arnolphe and signals the end of her attempts not to hurt his feelings (note her triple use of 'hélas' (1523; 1532; 1568) and the sympathetic question which immediately precedes Arnolphe's declaration: 'Du meilleur de mon cœur je voudrais vous complaire'). Ironically, her direct comment undermines the prospects of a marriage to Horace (as had happened with her ingenuous revelations in II, 5).

3) Comic irony pervades Arnolphe's outburst in 1607-11: his 'colère' (1569) has not been 'désarmée' for very long; 'bête trop indocile' recalls Chrysalde's warning in 107-108 of the dangers of marrying someone who was unaware of the distinctions between right and wrong; 'dénicherez' (which takes up 'mon pauvre petit bec') paints the incongruous picture of a protective mother about to drive the fledgling from the nest for its own good; the return to the convent brings us full circle (cf. the *maximes* and Agnès's education). Furthermore, the idea of claustration is for Arnolphe a means of punishment rather than a refuge or a place of meditation. The punishment 'un cul de convent' (= the darkest recess, the darkest dungeon) is incommensurate with the offence of her rejection of Arnolphe's 'vœux'. Here, read 'désirs amoureux' (though entrance to a convent usually entailed the taking of 'vœux' = marriage to Christ). Arnolphe's change of plan is ironically disguised as a continuation of his strategy: 'Je suivrai mon dessein' (in I, 1, his 'dessein' was to 'prendre femme'). The use of the future is again ill-chosen in view of the pre-arranged marriage which closes the play.

(iv) Conclusion

From the point of view of the plot, the passage reflects in microcosm the comic rhythm of the play, tracing the pendulum-type swing from confidence to humiliation. Both characters are reduced to despair: Arnolphe's is a double deflation of unreciprocated love and the confirmation of his fear of being cuckolded; and Agnès's expectations will be cruelly deceived by the banishment to a condition far worse than the one she was in at the beginning of the play. After this scene, no internal solution will be possible. The resolution of the dramatic problem, the marriage of the lovers, will be achieved by the device of the *patres ex machina* , the returning fathers who make their first appearance in the dénouement to divulge the conjugal arrangements.

The passage under review has frequently been perceived as tragic, not just by the Romantics and by Balzac's Maxime de Trailles—'Moi je pleure à la grande scène d'Arnolphe' (*Beatrix*)—but also by critics like Arnavon (pp. 297; 314), for whom this scene approaches serious drama: 'Le ton de la comédie est largement dépassé [...] L'effet comique, au demeurant, est, ici, secondaire. Ce qui compte, c'est le trouble de cette âme ravagée, dévastée, scalpée [...]'. Molière's intention of comedy is, however, confirmed by the evidence he has left us of his own performance of this scene and of the response of its first audiences:

> Et ce Monsieur de la Souche enfin, qu'on nous fait un homme d'esprit, et qui paraît si sérieux en tant d'endroits, ne descend-il point dans quelque chose de trop comique et de trop outré au cinquième acte, lorsqu'il explique à Agnès la violence de son amour, avec ces roulements d'yeux extravagants, ces soupirs ridicules, et ces larmes niaises qui font rire tout le monde? (*La Critique* , sc. 6)

Far from presenting Arnolphe as a 'pathetic victim of circumstances', the passage represents what Howarth has rightly called 'the climax of the comic portrayal of the central character ' (*3* , p. xvii).

Chapter Six

New Comedy

The comic war provoked by the play has left us a testament to Molière's originality. In judging the work by the conventional theories of the time, Molière's critics have paradoxically underlined for posterity his distinctive achievement. The literary polemic focused on four areas: (A) the mixture of *genres* ; (B) the portrayal of the comic hero; (C) the element of plagiarism; (D) the aim of comedy.

(A) THE MIXTURE OF *GENRES*

In seventeenth-century theory the separation between the different *genres* —in particular, between tragedy and comedy—was treated by the French as an almost inviolable rule. Shakespeare did not observe such distinctions with the same rigour; in some of his greatest tragedies there are elements of comedy. Molière does not, however, bring together tragedy and comedy in *L'Ecole des femmes* as has been alleged. This is to misapprehend the context in which Arnolphe's so-called tragic utterances are made and to take at face value the comic hero's self-assessment.

Molière does however blend two different types of comedy which were at the time regarded as very distinct: literary comedy and farce.

(i) Literary Comedy

Many of the five-act comedies of the first half of the century followed the erudite tradition of the Italian Renaissance, the *commedia erudita* or *sostenuta* (so called because they were humanist adaptations of plays by Plautus and Terence). Such plays were aimed at a mainly sophisticated audience. Sometimes called comedies of intrigue, these plays had convoluted plots often based on the lovers' struggle against stern (and usually miserly) fathers. The lovers were traditionally supported by servants or slaves, and the unravelling of the various plot complications was often effected by the discovery of the true identity of one or more of the characters in the final scene of the play.

The framework of *L'Ecole des femmes* is literary. The first scene features an ideological discussion, and the ending a recognition scene of the type mentioned above. The five-act verse form was also considered to be the most appropriate model for literary comedy (and indeed, for tragedy). In this respect, Molière was writing within the accepted tradition.

Molière's great innovation is to graft into the literary structure elements of the farce tradition. Two years before *L'Ecole des femmes* in 1660, Pierre Corneille had condemned such fusion. Writing about his first comedy *Mélite* (1629), he was critical of any concession he had made to popular taste. Comedy, for Corneille, entailed a 'peinture de la conversation des honnêtes gens', that is, the 'genteel portrayal of middle class life' (see Howarth, 22 , p. 77). Corneille's comedies tended to be refined, provoking a smile rather than laughter.

(ii) Farce

The farce tradition in seventeenth-century France had itself two distinct strands: the *commedia dell'arte* and native French farce. The *commedia* had been imported from Italy and had become very popular in the 1660s. Its plays were of one act or, at most, three acts. Called *scenarii*, they were largely plotless, consisting of a series of situations which allowed scope for improvisation and joke-telling on the part of the performers. Acting was physically expressive, akin to the modern circus or pantomime routines.

Roles were fixed, with the male characters wearing masks which identified them immediately for the audience: e.g. *Pantalone* , the miserly old man with the hooked nose and pointed beard, or the *Pedante* with his black gown and flat hat.

The native French Farce tradition, which derived from Medieval Farce, was perpetuated in the first quarter of the seventeenth century by Gros-Guillaume, Gaultier-Garguille, Turlupin, Bruscambille and Tabarin. Old French Farce differed from the *commedia* chiefly in its emphasis on social relationships, and, in particular, on conjugal strife. Plots often revolved around the ruses of scheming wives to cuckold their husbands. The farce tradition went out of fashion from 1642 onwards. As Scarron remarked in 1657 in *Le Roman comique* (though with characteristic exaggeration): 'Aujourd'hui la farce est abolie'.

Aspects of both farce traditions are found in *L'Ecole des femmes* . Old French Farce provides the cuckoldry theme; the peasant servants with French names (some of Molière's servants with origins in the *commedia* had Italianate names, like Mascarille); the ribald jokes on sexuality; the inadvertent confidences of Horace which, taken directly from Scarron's *La Précaution inutile* , have been shown to reflect a situation in Old French Farce entitled *Resjouy d'amours* . From the *commedia* are derived some of the *lazzi* (pieces of stage business), particularly the beatings, and stock types (Arnolphe has traits of *Pantalone* ; the Notaire is a development of the self-absorbed *Pedante*).

Some of the farcical elements caused a storm of protest in Molière's day. The elliptical 'le' was regarded as obscene; expressions like 'tarte à la crème', the equation of emotions and 'potage', and the anecdote about 'auricular conception' ('les enfants par l'oreille') were treated as an offence against the *bienséances* , the standards of seemliness of polite society. Molière's parody of his critics in *La Critique* , sc. 3 has left us an idea of the substance of the debate: 'Les *enfants par l'oreille* m'ont paru d'un goût détestable; la *tarte à la crème* m'a affadi le cœur et j'ai pensé vomir au *potage* [...] Ce *le* scandalise furieusement [...] Il a une obscénité qui n'est pas supportable'. Molière's critics failed to perceive the distinctive shape of

L'Ecole des femmes : the integration of Corneille's conception of literary comedy—the strictly non-laughable 'conversation des honnêtes gens'—with the farce tradition. Molière had begun his career as a dramatist by writing farces: the only two surviving *canevas* which have been attributed to him, *La Jalousie du Barbouillé* and *Le Médecin volant*, were modelled respectively on native French Farce and the *commedia*. His first two full-length plays, *L'Etourdi* (1655) and *Le Dépit amoureux* (1656), were constructed after the Italian literary tradition. *L'Ecole des femmes* is adumbrated in *Les Précieuses ridicules* (1659), which moves from a literary opening to a farcical ending. In *Les Précieuses* the 'conversation' is turned to ridicule on the lips of would-be 'honnêtes gens'. The formula which had been applied with great success to the one-act prose play is developed over five acts in verse in *L'Ecole des femmes*.

(B) THE COMIC HERO

The portrayal of Arnolphe has proved another source of contention. Two things in particular have fuelled the controversy: (i) the fusion of serious and farcical elements; (ii) the extent to which Arnolphe is a 'realistic' portrayal of a seventeenth-century bourgeois.

(i) A Hybrid Creation

Lysidas resumes the arguments of Molière's antagonists:

> Et puisque c'est le personnage ridicule de la pièce, fallait-il lui faire faire l'action d'un honnête homme? [...] Et ce Monsieur de la Souche enfin, qu'on nous fait un homme d'esprit, et qui paraît si sérieux en tant d'endroits, ne descend-il point dans quelque chose de trop comique et de trop outré au cinquième acte, lorsqu'il explique à Agnès la violence de son amour, avec ces roulements d'yeux extravagants, ces soupirs ridicules, et ces larmes niaises qui font rire tout le monde? (*La Critique*, sc. 6)

Arnolphe is not simply a punchbag or a pasteboard figure like the protagonists of the farce tradition. At the same time he lacks the dignity expected of a hero of the literary tradition (see Howarth, 22 , p. 121). Molière justifies the curious dichotomy through Dorante: 'il n'est pas incompatible qu'une personne soit ridicule en de certaines choses et honnête homme en d'autres' (sc. 6). Dorante's words reveal the make-up of Molière's comic figures. His monomaniacs are represented as worthy of respect and sympathy—where their particular fixation is not concerned. Such positive traits sharpen Molière's focus on the character's obsessiveness. In the case of Arnolphe, his preoccupation with cuckoldry is heightened by the positive qualities which emerge from the situations in which he has been placed: his being a man of the world and successful in business; his capacity for friendship, demonstrated in the long-established relationships with Chrysalde and Oronte; his generosity, seen in the spontaneous offer of money to the young lover. All of these potentially admirable qualities are however vitiated and distorted by Arnolphe's *idée fixe* : friendship with Chrysalde is sorely tested (note the breakdown in communication between Arnolphe and Chrysalde (I, 1 and V, 9); friendship for Horace turns to rivalry on Arnolphe's discovery of the purpose to which his money will be put; the renewal of the relationship with Oronte leads to Arnolphe's ultimate humiliation; Arnolphe's generosity descends to villainy.

(ii) "Realism"

Opinion is sharply divided on the extent to which Arnolphe is "true to life". Much of the confusion arises from remarks made by Dorante: 'lorsque vous peignez les hommes, il faut peindre d'après nature' (sc. 6). Dorante's elaboration of this guideline has ironically led to further confusion: 'On veut que ces portraits ressemblent; et vous n'avez rien fait, si vous n'y faites reconnaître les gens de votre siècle'. Dorante is however adopting an extreme position to correct an imbalance in his interlocutor, namely that Molière's type of comedy is trivial ('bagatelles') compared with the 'beauté des pièces sérieuses'.

Three misapprehensions still obtain. Firstly, that Arnolphe is a typical seventeenth-century bourgeois. De Visé attacked Molière for "slavish naturalism". Scholars have sought vainly for "real-life" models for Arnolphe. In any case, such an emphasis seems misplaced, denying the imaginative element in a work of art, and this approach is of interest mainly to the sociologist or historian or to the reporter like de Visé rather than to the student of literature—besides, Molière's sources have been found to be in theatrical and literary models. The second misapprehension is the equation of "realism" with the nineteenth-century movement dominated by Balzac. Apart from the anachronism, this equation ignores Molière's distortion of the social reality for comic effect. The third and most recent misunderstanding stems from attempts to interpret Molière's comic hero in the light of post-Freudian psychology: Arnolphe is made to suffer an "anal complex" and other deep-seated neuroses. This interpretation abstracts the character from the dramatic situation apart from which he has no existence, and gives a very sombre colouring to the play.

Molière's "new realism"—'peindre d'après nature'—can best be understood if we take into account dramaturgical rather than historical or psychological considerations. Molière does not provide us with an exact representation of his times, but with an imaginative portrayal of a man with a particular fixation. The mirror which Molière holds up to his society is essentially a comic mirror. As Howarth has observed (*21* , p. 5), this mirror is not 'a plain reflecting one which shows life as it is but something not unlike the distorting mirror of the fairground which turns us all into stylised thin men, fat ladies, giants or dwarfs'. Arnolphe is essentially an *imaginaire* , inhabiting a world of his own fantasy which contrasts with the "real" world of those he encounters—paradoxically, their "real" world is itself a theatrical one, distinct from the everyday reality of the audience. Molière's "new realism" derives therefore from his blending of the different comic traditions: the realistic imitation characteristic of literary comedy and the extravagant distortion of farce.

(C) PLAGIARISM

Molière was criticized by his contemporaries for lack of originality and for pillaging other works; his sources (particularly his borrowings from Scarron's *La Précaution inutile*) have been well explored. The charge of plagiarism cannot be refuted. It can, however, be justified, particularly in terms of the seventeenth-century's view of originality, which consisted more in the arrangement of material than in the material itself (see Broome, p. 22). What is important is not what Molière has taken, but what his dramatic imagination has achieved with his borrowings. Molière's originality lay in his fusion of disparate elements into a coherent whole.

(D) THE AIM OF COMEDY

The play was regarded by some contemporaries of Molière as socially and morally anarchic. Arnolphe's sermon was considered a parody of the Ten Commandments; the *scène du ruban* was adjudged scandalous; and de-stabilization of households was thought likely as a result of Agnès's disregard for (what was considered to be) established morality.

Molière's critics imputed to him a satiric intention in the play. This is difficult to prove, with nothing more than a *riposte* —in dramatic form—to guide us. Satirical references to the Corneille brothers—'Gros Pierre' and 'Monsieur de l'Isle' (179-82)—were first pointed out by the seventeenth-century drama critic d'Aubignac: the relationship between the Corneille brothers and Molière suffered considerably. There may have been a satiric intention, or the references could have been no more than a topos (see Hall, p. 142). The thesis that the play contains a satire of religion is more difficult to sustain. Admittedly, in a church state, in which deviations from the received tradition were punished with maximum rigour—Claude le Petit was burned for suspected atheism in 1662; religious dissidents like the Jansenists and Protestants were persecuted—Molière would not have confessed to any subversive attitudes. Yet Molière's defence gives an indication of aesthetic priorities (the coherence of the roles):

> Pour le discours moral que vous appelez un sermon, il est certain que de vrais dévots qui l'ont ouï n'ont pas trouvé qu'il choquât ce que vous dites; et sans doute que ces paroles d'*enfer* et de *chaudières bouillantes* sont assez justifiées par l'extravagance d'Arnolphe et par l'innocence de celle à qui il parle [...] . (*La Critique*, sc. 6)

Even Agnès's reported remarks about "auricular conception" may be viewed as an example of her innocence and ignorance: her fanciful belief could have been inspired by an ill-informed response to pictures of the Annunciation in the convent.

If there be any "satire" in the play, its function is paradoxical: to parody the created satirist, Arnolphe, who is eager to ridicule the mores of his contemporaries and to jot down on his *tablettes* details of any marital misfortune. The main focus is on Arnolphe's misapprehension of religion and not on the religion he corrupts; as in *Les Précieuses ridicules* and *Tartuffe*, the gap between the false and the real is the principal source of comedy. Hence the play transcends its immediate context. Contrast, for example, the lukewarm reception given to a repeat broadcast, after twenty years, of a satirical television programme (*That Was The Week That Was*) featuring political controversies: the item on the Profumo affair, stripped of its historical relevance, was scarcely comic.

However, it is to *La Critique* that we must turn for final confirmation that Molière's aim was aesthetic and not didactic. He saw the novelty of his comedy not simply as an endeavour to portray the 'conversation des honnêtes gens' on the stage, but also to make the 'honnêtes gens' in the audience laugh without feeling ridiculous. Through Dorante, he emphasizes the difficulty of this undertaking: 'c'est une étrange entreprise que celle de faire rire les honnêtes gens' (sc. 6). Molière's ideal spectators were not easily moved to laughter (Howarth, *22*, pp. 63-75), but here they were allowed to point the finger of superiority at the supposedly 'honnête homme', Arnolphe, who fails to live up to the required standards of speech and behaviour.

May the fastidious modern 'honnêtes gens' who think it beneath their dignity to laugh, and who spurn Molière's initiative, reflect upon the irony of Horace's 'mais vous n'en riez pas assez, à mon avis' (938). Modern-day audiences need no repeated invitations to laugh insincerely: box-office receipts, then as now, attest to the enduring success of Molière's 'étrange entreprise'.

Bibliography

I   *ŒUVRES COMPLETES*

1.   — ed. E. Despois et P. Mesnard, Paris, Hachette (Les Grands Ecrivains de la France), 1873-1900, 13 vols.
2.   — ed. G. Couton, Paris, Gallimard (Bibliothèque de la Pléiade), 1971, 2 vols.

II   SEPARATE EDITIONS OF *L'ECOLE DES FEMMES*

3.   — with *La Critique de L'Ecole des femmes* , ed. W.D. Howarth, Oxford, Blackwell, 1963.
4.   — ed. S. Rossat-Mignod, Paris, Editions sociales, 'Les Classiques du Peuple', 1964.
5.   — ed. G. Sablayrolles, Paris, Larousse, 1965.
6.   — ed. P. Cabanis, Paris, Bordas, 1968.
7.   — *suivie de la Critique de L'Ecole des femmes* , ed. Rosalyne Laplace, Paris, Comédie-Française, 1983.
8.   — with *L'Ecole des maris* , *La Critique de L'Ecole des femmes* , *L'Impromptu de Versailles* , ed. J. Serroy, Paris, Gallimard (Collection Folio), 1985.
9.   — ed. R. Duchêne, (Preface by M. Maréchal), Paris, Librairie générale française (Livre de Poche), 1986.

III   STUDIES ON *L'ECOLE DES FEMMES*

10.   Arnavon, J.   *'L'Ecole des femmes' de Molière* , Paris, Plon, 1936.

11.	Broome, J.H.	*'L'Ecole des femmes' and 'Le Misanthrope'*, London, Grant and Cutler, 1982.
12.	Butin, J.	*L'Ecole des femmes*, Paris, Hatier, coll. 'Profil d'une œuvre', 1984.

IV GENERAL STUDIES

13.	Bergson, H.	*Le Rire. Essai sur la signification du comique*, Paris, F. Alcan, 1900.
14.	Bray, R.	*Molière, homme de théâtre*, Paris, Mercure de France, 1954.
15.	Conesa, G.	*Le Dialogue moliéresque : étude stylistique et dramaturgique*, Paris, P.U.F., 1983.
16.	Eustis, A.	*Molière as Ironic Contemplator*, The Hague / Paris, Mouton, 1973.
17.	Fernandez, R.	*La Vie de Molière*, Paris, Gallimard, 1929.
18	Gaines, J.F.	*Social Structures in Molière's Theater*, Columbus, Ohio State University Press, 1984.
19.	Grene, N.	*Shakespeare, Jonson, Molière: the comic contract*, London, Macmillan, 1980.
20.	Hall, H.G.	*Comedy in Context, Essays on Molière*, Jackson, Univ. of Mississippi Press, 1984.
21.	Howarth, W.D. (ed.)	*Comic Drama. The European Heritage*, London, Methuen, 1978.
22.	Howarth, W.D.	*Molière. A Playwright and his Audience*, Cambridge, University Press, 1982.
23.	Hubert, J.D.	*Molière and the Comedy of Intellect*, Berkeley, Univ. of California Press, 1962.
24.	Knutson, H.C.	*Molière: An Archetypal Approach*, Toronto, Univ. of Toronto Press, 1976.
25.	Lawrence, F.L.	*Molière: The Comedy of Unreason*, New Orleans, Tulane University, 1968.

26.	McBride, R.	*The Sceptical Vision of Molière. A Study in Paradox*, London, Macmillan, 1977.
27.	McBride, R.	*Aspects of Seventeenth-Century French Drama and Thought*, London, Macmillan, 1979.
28.	Moore, W.G.	*Molière. A New Criticism*, Oxford, Clarendon Press, 1949.
29.	Truchet, J. (ed.)	*Thématique de Molière*, Paris, SEDES, 1985.

V   ARTICLES

30.	Albanese jr., R.	'Pédagogie et didactisme dans *l'Ecole des femmes*', *Romance Notes*, 16 (1974), 114-23.
31.	Barnwell, H.T.	'Molière's Language and the Expectation of Comedy', *Studi francesi*, 19 (1975), 34-47.
32.	Beck, W.	'Arnolphe ou Monsieur de la Souche', *French Review*, 42 (1968-69), 254-61.
33.	Berlan, Françoise	'L'ingénuité d'Agnès. Etude d'un champ lexical dans *L'Ecole des femmes*', *L'Information grammaticale*, 24 (jan. 1985), 20-27.
34.	Bonnard, H.	'Etude de langue et de style d'un passage de *L'Ecole des femmes*', *L'Information grammaticale*, 23 (oct.1984), 18-23.
35.	Clark, D.	'*L'Ecole des femmes* - Plotting and Significance in a 'Machine à Rire'', *Society for Seventeenth-Century French Studies*, XI (1989), 117-35.
36.	Conesa, G.	'Remarques sur la structure dramatique de *L'Ecole des femmes*', *Revue d'histoire du théâtre*, 30 (1978), 120-26.
37.	Dandrey, P.	'Structures et espaces de communication dans *L'Ecole des femmes*'. *Littérature*, 63 (1986), 65-89.

38.	Doubrovsky, S.	'Arnolphe ou la chute du héros', *Mercure de France*, 343 (1961), 111-118.
39	Eckstein, Nina	'Functions of the *Récit* in *L'Ecole des femmes*', *Kentucky Romance Quarterly*, 30 (1983), 223-30.
40.	Emelina, J.	'*L'Ecole des femmes* et le pittoresque', *Hommage à Claude Digeon*, Paris, Les Belles Lettres (Publications de la Faculté des lettres et sciences humaines de Nice, N° 36), pp. 41-49.
41.	Fraser, R.D. and Rendell, S.F.	'The Recognition Scenes in Molière's Theater', *Romanic Review*, 64 (1973), 16-31.
42.	Gutwirth, M.	'Arnolphe et Horace', *L'Esprit créateur*, VI, 3 (1966), 188-96.
43.	Gutwirth, M.	'Molière and the Woman Question: *Les Précieuses ridicules*, *L'Ecole des femmes*, *Les Femmes savantes*', *Théâtre Journal*, 34 (1982), 345-59.
44.	Hampshire, P.	'Introduction to Molière's *L'Ecole des femmes*', *Modern Languages*, LXIII (1982), 215-21.
45.	Herzel, R.W.	'The Décor of Molière's Stage: the testimony of Brissart and Chauveau', *Publications of the Modern Language Association of America*, XCIII, 5 (1978), 925-54.
46.	Hope, Q.	'Animals in Molière', *Publications of the Modern Language Association of America*, LXXIX (1964), 411-21.
47.	Johnson, Barbara	'Teaching ignorance: *L'Ecole des femmes*', *Yale French Studies*, 63 (1982), 165-82.
48.	Kern, Edith	'*L'Ecole des femmes* and the Spirit of Farce', *L'Esprit créateur*, XIII, 3 (1973), 220-28.
49.	Knutson, H.C.	'Comedy as a "School": the Beginnings of a Title Form', *Australian Journal of French Studies*, XX, 1 (1983), 3-14.
50.	Letts, J.T.	'*L'Ecole des femmes* ou la défaite de la parole inauthentique', *Modern Language Notes*, 95 (1980), 1023-32.

51.	Magne, B.	'L'Ecole des femmes ou la conquête de la parole', *Revue des sciences humaines*, 145 (1972), 125-40.
52.	Nelson, R.J.	'Molière: the Metaphysics of Comedy', *L'Esprit créateur*, XV (1975), 119-29.
53.	Nicolich, R.N.	'Door, Window and Balcony in *L'Ecole des femmes*', *Romance Notes*, 12 (1970-71), 364-69.
54.	Peacock, N.A.	'Verbal Costume in *L'Ecole des femmes*', *The Modern Language Review*, 79, 3 (1984), 541-52.
55.	Picard, R.	'Molière comique ou tragique? Le cas Arnolphe', *Revue d'histoire littéraire de la France*, 72 (1972), 769-85.
56.	Porter, H.D.	'Comic Rhythm in *L'Ecole des femmes*', *Forum for Modern Language Studies*, 5 (1969), 205-17.
57.	Powell, J.	'Making Faces. Character and Physiognomy in *L'Ecole des femmes* and *L'Avare*', *Society for Seventeenth-Century French Studies*, IX (1987), 94-112.
58.	Serroy, J.	'Le petit chat est mort ...', *Recherches et travaux*, 28 (1985), 79-91.
59.	Slater, Maya	'Molière's Women - a Matter of Focus', *Themes in Drama II : Women in Theatre*, ed. J. Redmond, Cambridge, University Press, 1989, pp. 75-85.
60.	Tobin, R.W.	'Les Mets et les mots: gastronomie et sémiotique dans *L'Ecole des femmes*', *Semiotica*, 1984, 133-45.
61.	Weinberg, B.	'Plot and Thesis in *L'Ecole des femmes*', *Romance Notes*, 15, Suppl. Nº 1 (1973), 78-97.
62.	Zwillenberg, Myrna K.	'Arnolphe, Fate's Fool', *The Modern Language Review*, 68 (1973), 292-308.

VI   TAPES

63.   Chaplin, Peggy   *L'Ecole des femmes*, Exeter, 1979.